This is a book about bread, how to make it and how to eat it at every stage of its life cycle. It's a revival of cucina povera (poverty cooking)—a bread-centric approach to meal prep that has fallen out of favor in American kitchens and that James Beard Award–nominated baker Rick Easton is hell-bent on restoring.

In these pages, you'll find everything you need for baking your own bread (although you could just frequent your local bakery, as people have done for thousands of years); things to make with bread (Bread Meatballs! Pasta with Bread Crumbs and Cauliflower!); things to eat with bread (Greens and Beans! Dried Chestnut and White Bean Soup!); and, of course, the ultimate guide to sandwiches you never knew you needed (Tuna with Harissa, Eggs, and Olives! Frittata, Artichoke, Pecorino, and Mint!) A mostly Italian celebration of bread in all its forms—from fresh-baked to stale, from slices to crumbs—*Bread and How to Eat It* is an eminently accessible, riotously opinionated, and utterly indispensable cookbook for making the most of every loaf.

Bread

AND HOW TO EAT IT

Bread

AND HOW TO EAT IT

RICK EASTON

with MELISSA McCART

Photography by Johnny Fogg

ALFRED A. KNOPF NEW YORK 2023

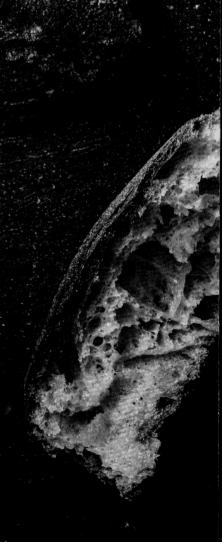

THIS IS A BORZOI BOOK
PUBLISHED BY ALFRED A. KNOPF

www.aaknopf.com

Knopf, Borzoi Books, and the colophon are registered
trademarks of Penguin Random House LLC.

Library of Congress Cataloging-in-Publication Data
Names: Easton, Rick, author. | McCart, Melissa, author. |
  Fogg, Johnny, photographer.
Title: Bread and how to eat it / Rick Easton with Melissa McCart ;
  photography by Johnny Fogg.
Description: First edition. | New York : Alfred A. Knopf, 2023. | Includes
  index. | Summary: "75 Italian(ish) recipes for baking, using, and eating with
  bread, from the owner of the bakery Bread & Salt"— Provided by publisher.
Identifiers: LCCN 2022009002 (print) | LCCN 2022009003 (ebook) |
  ISBN 9780593319093 (hardcover) | ISBN 9780593319109 (ebook)
Subjects: LCSH: Cooking, Italian. | Bread. | Bread & Salt Bakery (New Jersey)
Classification: LCC TX723 .E26 2023 (print) | LCC TX723 (ebook) |
  DDC 641.5945—dc23/eng/20220520
LC record available at https://lccn.loc.gov/2022009002
LC ebook record available at https://lccn.loc.gov/2022009003

Some of the recipes in this book may include raw eggs, meat, or fish. When
these foods are consumed raw, there is always the risk that bacteria, which is
killed by proper cooking, may be present. For this reason, when serving these
foods raw, always buy certified salmonella-free eggs and the freshest meat
and fish available from a reliable grocer, storing them in the refrigerator until
they are served. Because of the health risks associated with the consumption
of bacteria that can be present in raw eggs, meat, and fish, these foods should
not be consumed by infants, small children, pregnant women, the elderly, or
any persons who may be immunocompromised. The author and publisher
expressly disclaim responsibility for any adverse effects that may result from
the use or application of the recipes and information contained in this book.

Jacket photograph by Johnny Fogg
Jacket design by Kelly Blair

Manufactured in China
First Edition

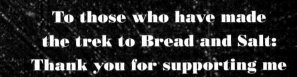

To those who have made
the trek to Bread and Salt:
Thank you for supporting me

Contents

Sandwiches

Pieces

Meatballs and "meatballs"

Crumbs

Things to Eat with Bread

Breakfast Cereal and Sweets

Introduction

We live in a time when there are bakeries producing high-quality bread in more places in the United States, and possibly worldwide, than ever before in our lifetime. This isn't just true of large cities on the coasts; there are many bakers across the country laboring to provide better bread for their communities.

The rise of the internet and social media has dramatically increased the sharing of knowledge about baking and bread among novices and professionals alike. The coronavirus pandemic led to an increased interest in home baking, as many people have had more time at home. Meanwhile, sales at bakeries across the country have risen significantly. Suddenly, everyone has at least some cursory knowledge of sourdough, and low-carbohydrate diets of all kinds seem to be on the wane.

This increased interest in bread and bread-making is positive overall, but, like so many trends fueled by social media, it has also created a culture of imitation severed from any historic, cultural, or geographic context. Both home bakers and professionals often strive for a fashionable, visually stunning, modern style of open-crumb bread. While photos of this style of bread give some indication of texture, they say nothing about its flavor, aroma, or place on the table.

This fetishization of how bread looks stems from an extreme privilege that ignores the essential role bread plays in the lives of millions of people across the world. Many people need bread to survive, or at least to make sure that they don't go hungry.

The modern world is a strange place, and we in America are a strange people. People may line up around the block to buy bread from popular bakeries, but they are often disconnected from the fundamentally humble and quotidian nature of the product. They are often at a loss as to what to do with a loaf of bread much beyond making a sandwich or a piece of toast.

I remember when I was a gluttonous little kid and I'd sit down at a restaurant and the server would put down a basket of bread on the table. I'd start eating the bread, and my parents and grandparents would say, "Don't fill up on bread, because we're going to have all this other food. We're going to order other things. Don't spoil your appetite."

As an adult, I have a very different perspective. With the caveat that I am not a dietitian or a doctor, I would tell you that you *should* fill up on bread, for a couple of reasons. First, much of the world plans their meals around bread of some kind; you're in good company. Second, if you're eating bread as a fundamental part of your diet, you can likely afford to spend more money on better and more nutritious ingredients for the other food you eat.

Take the grapefruit salad on page 177, for example. If you have beautiful in-season grapefruit and some new-crop olive oil, and use a nice piece of bread to sop up all those juices and everything else that is left on the plate, that in and of itself makes a meal. Don't think of bread as a separate component, like a side in a meat-n-three. It is integral to the meal, as woven into it as seasonings or herbs.

I believe that you should eat good food—with bread serving as both a foundation and a complement. This is even more appropriate now in the face of a changing global economy, as wealth concentrates in the hands of fewer people and it becomes harder for poor people to eat well. As someone who has intermittently not had a bank account, I count myself among them. Seeing the direction the world has been sliding toward since the eighties has helped shape my career path to become a baker. Feeding people good food, unprocessed food, bread that's not made with garbage that harms your health—it can be a quietly revolutionary act.

People may line up around the block to buy bread from popular bakeries, but they are often disconnected from the fundamentally humble and quotidian nature of the product. They are often at a loss as to what to do with a loaf of bread much beyond making a sandwich or a piece of toast.

Our ancestors knew the importance of eating bread as a primary part of their meals, and they often had to use stale bread as well as fresh in times of hardship. I think there's both value and pleasure to be had in using bread in a creative way to form the basis of a healthy diet. In any event, it's how I eat, and I find that I eat better than most people, using better ingredients that cost far less.

If you're eating bread as a fundamental part of your diet, you can likely afford to spend more money on better and more nutritious ingredients for the other food you eat.

This book is about bread. It's about how to eat it. It's about what to do with it beyond toasting it or making a sandwich with it when it's fresh and then letting it go stale and putting it in the trash. This is a book for those people who come to my store, Bread and Salt, every week and say, "I can't get a whole loaf of bread. It's too big. It will go bad." It's a book to help broaden people's appreciation of bread, and what goes into making it.

I am going to teach you what to look for when you're buying bread, how to store it, and how to use it when it's fresh and when it's old. I'm going to show you how you can eat bread; how bread can save you money; and how bread isn't just something that comes before dinner, served in a basket.

When I first got really into cooking, I was very interested in the foods of the Middle East and North Africa, and in cooking and eating food from that part of the world; I fell in love with the bread as well as simple dishes made from great ingredients.

The first time I ate truly good bread was in southern Morocco, where there's still a strong tradition of women making dough in their homes with hamira beldieh (natural yeast or, more literally, local or country yeast). They take the dough to their community bakeries, the baker loads the small rounds into a wood-fired firin (oven), and they sell the baked bread on the street.

As I got more into baking, I traveled throughout the Mediterranean into Sicily and southern Italy, a region that had been dominated by Arabic peoples for a very long time.

On my first trip to Italy—which wasn't that long ago—I was excited by the wide range of bread and baking techniques used in that country alone. While you'd find some mass-market breads in every province, the country still has a vibrant culture of regional bread baking, and it is important to Italians' cultural identity.

My interest in Sicily and southern Italy was also shaped by my own upbringing in Pittsburgh, where Italian Americans are a big part of public culture and life. This is why so much of what I cook is Italian: the efficiency, economy, and frugality of a traditional Italian kitchen and the role that bread has on the table is very moving to me.

When I returned to the States, I went looking for good bread, and I couldn't find any. The realization pushed me to dedicate myself to baking. I started with a CSA baking business in Charlottesville, Virginia, followed by an underground restaurant out of my house, where I first started serving meals with bread at the center, from polpetti di pane and cabbage salad to pancotto with beans.

But baking from home wasn't, and isn't, ideal. I lined the floor of my oven with brick in a ridiculous effort to increase its thermal mass and simulate a hearth. I built fires inside the oven to make pizzas, which was really dumb—and a disaster. (I ended up melting off all of the plastic knobs that controlled the gas, and learned that's not how brick ovens work.)

By 2013, I wanted to open a storefront, so I went back home to Pittsburgh—primarily because I didn't have much money and the rents were cheap, and the city was in the middle of a revival. I opened Bread and Salt with $60,000 in a one-story building that used to be a slaughterhouse. It was tucked away on a side street in Bloomfield, an Italian neighborhood that had bustled in Pittsburgh's heyday. I idealistically hoped to change what people expected from a loaf of bread, to help them realize that a staple of an everyday diet could be remarkable.

Then, in 2019, my cheese purveyor and friend Rynn Caputo, of Caputo Brothers Creamery in Pennsylvania, arranged an important meeting for me in Jersey City. Some of her restaurant friends there had found me a space in a former pizzeria across from a park with a view

The efficiency, economy, and frugality of a traditional Italian kitchen and the role that bread has on the table is very moving to me.

of Manhattan. It had an outdoor area in the back and a garage door in the front that opened onto the sidewalk. The basement prep area was huge. They wanted me to move Bread and Salt to the Garden State. I had never even been to New Jersey, but it was a great opportunity, and I couldn't say no. (Melissa, my partner and the coauthor of this book, is from New Jersey, which helped with the decision.)

People ask me why I've focused on the food of southern Italy and Sicily in particular. I've been fascinated by ancient recipes and cooking methods since I became interested in cooking. I'm self-taught, but since both my parents are professors and I had studied history, it's been a natural extension of my interests to go down rabbit holes that took me to books like Pellegrino Artusi's *Science in the Kitchen and the Art of Eating Well.* Many of the old Italian recipes I admire can be found in the Middle East and Greece as well. In Beatrice Ughi, founder of Italian product importer Gustiamo, I found a guide who introduced me to farmers and millers and purveyors who make quality ingredients that I am passionate about. Though her business is based in the Bronx, Beatrice has supported me through every stage of my business and has given me access to knowledge that I would not have likely have stumbled upon myself.

This book is an amalgam of recipes I have made at Bread and Salt, as well as others I make for entertaining and at home. They are celebrations of bread, even if it's something you'd eat on the side. It's a road map of how I cook and eat. Even if it doesn't turn your culinary world upside down, I hope it offers you moments of inspiration in terms of how you spend money on ingredients, how you cook, and how you derive pleasure when it comes to feeding yourself and the people you love.

My approach to bread

Bread should not be an afterthought

Whether you're baking your own bread or not, odds are that *most* of the bread you eat comes from outside your home. So it's helpful to know something about it.

Buying bread should require more thought than just throwing something into a grocery basket during a one-stop shop. Bread is worth going out of your way for. It's worth finding a bakery to frequent so you can develop a relationship with a local baker.

Your baker will help you better understand what makes good bread. If they're knowledgeable, you'll be introduced to a range of varieties from around the world, to be used for different occasions. In buying these loaves, you'll taste days where the conditions for bread baking are just right as well as days when they aren't. These experiences will help you fine-tune your palate.

Here's a framework for identifying good bread.

Bread is an expression of form . . .

Bread is made in a wide variety of shapes. By taking note of the shape, you can better understand whether it's an industrially produced loaf or made with attention to the craft. Is it elongated or round? Square or baked in a pan? Some strange whimsical shape? Something more free-form?

Customers tend to buy bread based on form. They go to the bakery and look for types they recognize, such as baguettes, ciabatta, and Pullman loaves. That's because they're buying bread for a purpose.

We can close our eyes and imagine the characteristics of a baguette, for example, because a baguette is defined by its form. A baguette is a certain length, whether it's a good baguette or a lousy one, a naturally fermented baguette or a yeasted loaf. There's a method of making a baguette, and bakers are, first and foremost, trying to achieve certain characteristics related to appearance and crust.

But there's way more to bread than its shape. There's the exterior and interior and texture of each—what's known, respectively, as the crust and the crumb. To evaluate bread, we have to slow down and use our senses.

Let's start with the crust. A good crust helps preserve the bread. The crust protects the interior and keeps it from drying out. When you keep bread on your counter, the crust is exposed to the air, and that's okay. It's already dry. It's a protective shell.

How to choose a bakery

Can you find good bread at a grocery store? I'd say no, but I'm not going to argue you out of your preferences. Maybe what you can find is fine. If you're not confident about buying bread, and you'd like to buy better bread, though, I'm here to help you.

When you enter a bakery, look at the bread selection. What is the style? What kinds of breads are displayed? Are they baked on-site? What color are the loaves? You can choose whatever style and color you like—but it's worth paying attention to variety, textures, and flavors to help shape your palate and your preference.

Develop a relationship with your local bakers and ask them questions about how they bake or how they achieve certain characteristics. Shop during both the bakery's peak and off-peak hours. Go back again and again. Get to know the people who work there. Most places will try to educate employees to answer basic customer questions. If you like bread, a bakery that will help you learn more is a good place to start.

When you buy a loaf of bread, consider the color of the crust. Is it blond or brown or reddish? Are there gradients of color? Slow, cold fermentation (to lower the temperature during the first or second rise) allows the conversion of more of the starch to sugar, which allows for caramelization and a Maillard reaction, which gives the crust its rich, honey color or mahogany hues.

When you see smooth, pale breads, it's often the result of a very fast process, baked at a low temperature or for a short amount of time. The texture of the crust has to do with whether it's a short, fast bake or long and slow; how hydrated the dough was; and how steam was used during baking. Sensually speaking, a nice crust provides you with a range of texture and flavor. The contrast between a crisp crust and a soft interior is one of the most beautiful parts of eating bread.

Let's move on to the crumb. Buy a decent bread knife. Always slice your own bread at home. Why? Because as soon as you slice bread, it starts to dry out. So why buy bread that's already dried out?

Here's why there are holes in the crumb of your bread. When you bake bread, the yeast releases the gas and water that is trapped in the gluten, creating steam, which leads to holes and bubbles. If the cell walls of the bubbles in the crumb are very thick, it can be an indication of improper development or underfermentation. You want the cell walls to be thin, with lots of little bubbles that make for a softer crumb and offer less resistance to your teeth. Large, irregular bubbles aren't inherently bad, but they can result from shaping defects or the bread being underproofed, or if the yeast hasn't produced enough carbon dioxide, which gives dough volume. Look inside and around the bubbles: they can give you a clearer picture of what's going on during fermentation.

The holes also have to do with the kinds and ratios of flours used; the consistency of the fermentation conditions (like temperature); and how the dough is handled and each loaf has been formed. Rough handling can de-gas, or flatten the dough, making bread more dense. But bread with small, tight holes isn't necessarily bad; it just depends on what type of bread you're buying. Rye bread, for example, is not going to have lots of holes. Some whole-grain bread will not have a wildly open crumb with an irregular structure.

Consider the characteristics when you cut open a loaf of bread. Is it white, yellow, or cream-colored? Is it brown or beige? Darker interiors are a sign of whole grain, which means more nutrients.

. . . and technique

How you shape a loaf requires a particular technique. You can't shape a baguette the way you shape a boule.

For every bread, bakers marshal a series of techniques to achieve the qualities they desire: the choice of flour(s); the type of leavening; the way dough is mixed; considerations of temperature, method, duration, and style of fermentation; how or whether a bread is scored; the temperature and duration of baking; the method of baking; and even how a bread is cooled and stored. All these decisions influence the characteristics of the finished bread.

Bakers don't use the same approach to make a ciabatta as they would a bagel. A loaf of 100 percent rye has to be handled differently than a 100 percent whole-wheat loaf.

Sometimes technique isn't deliberate, but comes about out of necessity—from a lack of time or resources, for example. Bread-making technique is hard enough to master, thanks to the myriad variables among flours, milling, and fermentation styles. But not having access to the right equipment makes it even more challenging, and it's a reason why the artisan baking renaissance has been a gradual one.

. . . and culture

All forms and techniques for making bread arise from distinct times and places. Bread is made in ways that serve specific communities and often hold religious or even political significance. The fact that most Americans eat mass-produced bread and may have trouble finding bread made with fresh-milled, regional grain is the result of the relationship between government and industrialized agriculture, advances in technology, and the values of

Slicing and storing bread

I'm telling you: Do not buy bread that's pre-sliced. This dries out the bread, and you're shortening its life cycle.

Whether it's cheap or expensive, buy a bread knife. But know that although higher-priced knives take longer to go dull, they will go dull, too. Look for a long blade to cut through larger loaves of bread. When you buy it, pay attention to how the handle feels in your hand. Too flimsy a blade is dangerous. You want one that's sharp enough to get through the crust easily without tearing the crumb.

While you can cut a loaf on a variety of surfaces, wood feels more natural to me, but if you use a plastic cutting board, it won't affect the life span of the knife.

Good bread doesn't go bad. Just store it in a dry place, like on your counter or on a cutting board, cut side down. You'll be able to slice it for a couple of days; after that, turn leftovers and crumbs into a hearty meal.

producing more for less—at any cost—over preserving craft or regional ingredients and cuisine.

In much of the rest of the world, people eat certain breads at certain times. There are occasions for fresh bread and for dried-out bread. Bread is treated with reverence. That's not as common in the United States, where we have never had a unified bread culture, but rather one that has been defined by waves of immigrants who make do with the ingredients they can find and afford.

Fashions and fads also factor into bread culture, which brings us to the anti-bread movement stemming from the popularity of paleo and other low-carb diets. I think cutting bread and carbs is silly and strips us of culture and pleasure. Chances are if you're reading this book, you're not anti-bread.

A baker can make a perfectly shaped bread with spot-on technique, but if you're part of a community, and you're baking to serve that community, you're often making bread that resonates with the culture of that community.

. . . and agriculture

Remember that bread is fundamentally an agricultural product. True, it's not a tomato or any other farm-grown product in the sense that a farmer tends to it and then sells it at a market. But in most parts of the country, bakeries are inspected by the U.S. Department of Agriculture. That's because a farmer grows the grain, that grain is milled, and the flour is turned into bread.

In this moment, most bakers are still removed from the fresh product at local bakeries, even when they're making an artisan product. There are very few bakers who have a relationship with farmers or millers or know what kinds of grain varieties they're using. But that's starting to change. For fairly large millers like King Arthur or Utah's Central Milling Company, the chief value in a bag of flour is its consistency. These mills pride themselves on being super reliable. But what if we thought of bread in terms of terroir, like wine?

The same farmer can plant the same variety of wheat on two separate pieces of land, with both plots treated the same and subjected to identical weather conditions. Yet he can produce two entirely different harvests—not just in terms of yields, but in terms of the flavor and performance of the wheat. Generally speaking, large mills source far and wide to find wheat that meets specific criteria, and they often blend a variety of wheat from a number of farms (and potentially even different harvests) to arrive at a consistent product.

Production bakeries—those that sell wholesale and supply many stores or restaurants—depend on this consistency; the operation doesn't work without it. In the past, a bad wheat harvest in a given area meant that people ate bad bread, or there was famine, or they ate corn, or chestnuts, or barley, or buckwheat, or whatever they could find. Baking was far more closely tied to the surrounding landscape.

Could you imagine a baker explaining to his customers, "I'm sorry the bread is really terrible. We've had a bad year for wheat"? Or, "Sorry, I am only making this weird chestnut bread this year." Probably not. Even the most fiercely committed bakers using local grain can just search farther afield to find better wheat when a bad season hits their area. It's great that we don't have to eat bad wheat now, but we have lost diversity, nutritional value, and

As your loaf ages

Once a loaf of bread has reached the second or third day, or a week—it depends on the condition the bread is in, and that varies according to how it was made and stored—I often cut it into slices and tear some of the slices into pieces and store them in a paper grocery bag that I leave open. That way, the pieces will continue to dry, and I can use them as they are or turn them into bread crumbs. I encourage you to do the same.

But if you have pets, like our Springer Spaniel, keep the bag out of reach. For whatever reason, animals love naturally leavened bread and assume that pieces are treats. Perhaps this is another use for old bread, but not one that I'm advocating here.

flavor in exchange for predictability, consistency, and security. This is more of a loss than we know.

When people ask me what kind of flour they should use, it's a challenging question to answer. What kind of bread are you trying to make? What kind of flour is available to you where you live? I want people to at least imagine what different kinds of grains in different kinds of places are like and how they're connected to a culture and landscape. In Castelvetrano, Sicily, miller extraordinaire Filippo Drago talks about how wild chamomile and fennel grow in between the wheat plants and add these perfumes to the grain, giving the finished bread all of the aromas of "il campo"—the country.

He isn't wrong. It's pretty remarkable. We don't often think about things like that in America, because we have farms that are thousands and thousands of acres growing modern hybrid wheat bred to only reach a certain height to prevent lodging (when it falls over) so it's easier to harvest with machines. When we think of wheat in America, we think of amber waves of grain. We think of the Midwest. We think of this endless prairie of monoculture abundance, and it doesn't reflect that there are varieties that have been selected throughout the years for whatever reasons, in particular locations and particular climates and soils that are different and have a sense of place.

How to use this book

Although most of the recipes in this book are Italian, it isn't an Italian cookbook. I am not Italian, and I do not present this collection of recipes as authoritative, comprehensive, or exhaustive. First and foremost, these are bread-centered recipes that I have learned about through traveling and eating and conversations and reading and mostly by making them again and again, either at Bread and Salt or at home. But most of them do come from Italy—because Italians, in particular, honor their bread.

I'd love for you to approach the recipes in this book with a sensitivity to the ingredients that you're working with. If something's coming out more dry than it should, add more liquid; if something's less dry, add less liquid. Not all bread is the same, which is also true as it ages. You have to use your judgment. You have to build experience through making things often and learning from each attempt. Very much like baking itself, you have to learn what the end result looks like and feels like and smells like and tastes like at different steps of the process and how to make adjustments as you need to.

xxiv

If you want to make your own bread, knock yourself out. My basic bread recipe is on page 8. Personally, I think people who bake bread at home are nuts: It's time-consuming. It's inefficient. Home ovens aren't designed to bake bread. The way to get good at making bread means baking again and again and again—which can get expensive. Baking bread at home is like riding a bike on bent rims: you can do it, but most of us wouldn't.

Plus, why make your own when you can buy something great from your local bakery, as people have for thousands of years? Whether you're using bread you made or bread you bought, however, this book is your guide for what to do with it, from more familiar uses (like sandwiches and toasts) to uses for bread that has gone stale (like pastas, vegetable dishes, and desserts). I've also included a selection of my favorite things to eat with bread (page 164), natural pairings because culturally they've always been served with bread. In that section in particular, keep in mind that bread can also extend the value of a meal—it's less expensive, albeit more modest, to eat beans with bread than to add a hunk of meat, for example. Especially if you're buying bread made by an excellent baker (or if you are that baker) using quality grains, a bowl of beans with bread is better for the environment and your health than, say, adding a slab of bacon or other kind of meat.

Finally, you'll see that some of the recipes are in narrative form. I don't want to overwrite extremely simple recipes where exact measurements aren't necessary. In fact, they're not really recipes—they're ideas. They're a conversation. When I'm at home, I don't gram things out like they do in professional kitchens (and I barely do it in my professional kitchen). These narratives are closer to how I cook. Don't worry about making mistakes. Allow yourself to freewheel and improvise. Have fun with them.

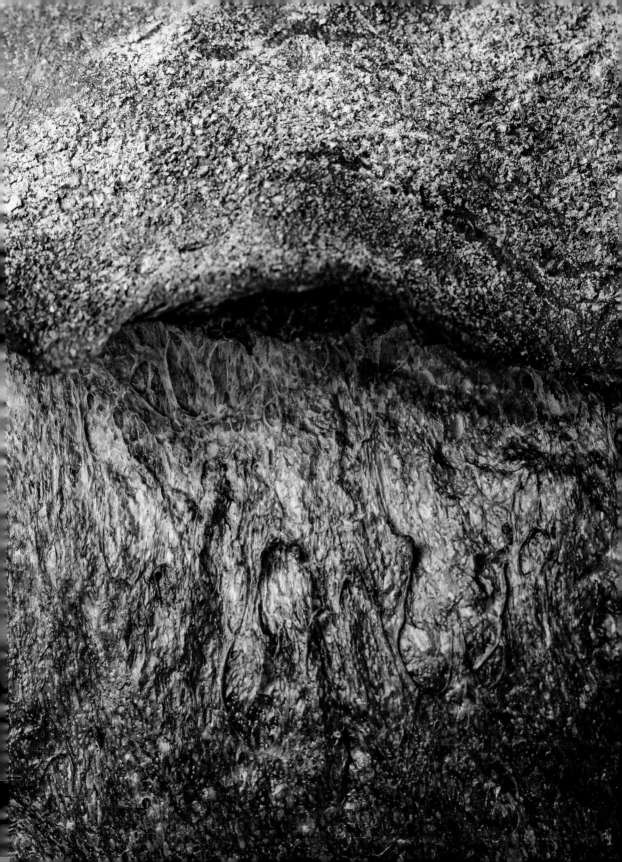

Essential Ingredients

These are the ingredients I use most; since they're basic staples, so will you. Because they're such fundamentals and such building blocks, people often take them for granted. You shouldn't. These are ingredients you need to pay close attention to.

Flour

How I buy flour depends on what I'm using it for—whether I'm making bread or pastry, or if I'm using it to flour something before breading and frying. I also buy different flours for different kinds of breads.

My advice is to use organic flour if you can afford it. Roundup is nasty. In the case of nonorganic wheat—if you don't have some assurance that the wheat hasn't been treated—the pesticides and/or fungicides can be ground up with the wheat berries, and you'll be eating it.

For many types of bread and other purposes, I prefer stone-milled flour. My personal favorites have a lot of the coarse bran sifted out, but all of the germ—where the nutrients are—is retained. Known as "high-extraction" flour, it's not as heavy as a true whole-grain flour, but it has a lot of the complexity of flavor and still has a lot of life in it. (See Resources, page 225.)

If you are new to baking bread, start with something reliable from a larger mill, like King Arthur, Bob's Red Mill, or Central Milling. High-protein bread flour is really strong and easy to work with and can take a lot of water, but most all-purpose flour can be used to make very good bread as well. As you get more comfortable with the process of bread making and more fluid in your handling of dough, start experimenting with more stone-milled and whole-grain flours, flours from smaller mills near where you live, and alternative grains.

I was once told that there is no such thing as bad flour, only bad bakers. This idea has tormented me over the years—especially at times when I struggled to make good bread from small mills producing flour from local wheats that maybe had too much enzymatic activity, had suffered too much starch damage in the milling process, had a low fermentation tolerance or mixing tolerance, or had any number of other problems. Through years of experience, good bakers have a relationship with and understanding of flour that allows them to make a number of adjustments in their process to compensate for various issues with a particular batch. They also know the kind of bread they want to make, and select the flours and techniques to help them achieve those results. Certainly, not all flours are suited for all types of bread. The very best bakers have the knowledge and understanding to guide each type of grain and flour to its highest expression. Begin your relationship with flours by getting to know as many as you can.

Salt

Salt comes from the sea or from places where the sea used to be. I use regular salt for any and all cooking and baking. In addition to providing salinity, salts have a pleasing minerality and lend an overall better flavor to food. I suggest keeping salts of various textures on hand. Try salts from different seas to see which you prefer and how they work with your cooking. Find the least-refined products you can and make sure they do not contain anti-caking agents so you're dealing with just salt, period.

Now, I know that a lot of culinary professionals insist that kosher salt is the only way to go. It's what most pros use. It's the only salt that lets you provide true, even seasoning. It just provides salinity and no other flavor that might interfere with the taste of the food. The shape and flake size of kosher salt makes it easy to grab a pinch, sprinkle it on your food, and achieve even seasoning.

The bad news is that kosher salt is close to 100 percent sodium chloride, providing a pure salinity that is possible only through chemical refinement.

All salt is made through a process of evaporation. I believe the trace elements of other minerals enhance—rather than interfere with—the flavor of food. One reason the pros swear by kosher salt is because it is relatively cheap, and the salt companies that created it have great marketing. Everyone has gotten used to it, and it has become the standard, at least in the U.S. Regular salt is more expensive than kosher salt, while mass-produced products like kosher salt are designed to be cheap.

For all these reasons, I do not use kosher salt, ever.

Salt might be the most important ingredient in your kitchen. Select one you like, stick with it, and use it with care.

Garlic

Choose garlic as you would in-season tomatoes, peppers, or eggplant. If you live in the Northeast, buy garlic in the spring and fall and try to get it from someone you know. Never buy pre-peeled garlic: it's done with chemicals, and it smells and tastes horrible. (Let's not even talk about pre-chopped garlic.) Keep in mind that different garlic varieties are better or worse for long-term storage. Just pay attention to how well it's cured, if it's cured at all, and how long it can be stored.

Eggs

You should buy eggs from a farmer in your community. The size is up to you—which is why I don't offer specifics about egg size for most of these recipes. I love vivid dark yolks, the color of marigolds. But more than anything else, I judge by taste and smell. Eggs that aren't very good have a funny smell to them and they weep—the whites are not firm. You might have to eat some less than great eggs before you find ones to love.

Tomatoes

With very few exceptions, they grow better tomatoes in Italy, where there are different soils, different climates, different traditions, different varieties. I like tomatoes that have certain acidity levels, savory qualities, textures, and choose them depending on how I'm going to use them. I like a little minerality, sometimes even bitterness. In Italy more than anywhere else, tomatoes are generally produced and grown by people who know what they're doing, who care, who put a lot of effort into them—and these are small producers.

I use plum varieties of tomatoes for pizza and meatballs. I don't always use San Marzano varieties. For one thing, they're expensive. For another, for pizza and meatballs, I prefer to use tomatoes that are slightly more acidic and have a deeper savory quality. They are a little less wet and can stand up to cooking. I use smaller varieties of plum tomatoes for quick cooking.

Anchovies

For our purposes, we're talking about salted anchovies. I seek out whole anchovies because I find them to be generally higher quality; the ones packed in oil are muddy-tasting and too soft.

Rinse them under cool running water and rub off the salt. Pick off their little fins. Open them by running your thumb down the belly, then run your thumb down the spine along the side then pull out the spine. Give them a final rinse and then pat them dry with paper towels. If I'm going to use them right away, they're ready to go. If I'm preparing them to use later, I'll soak them in a little bit of white wine for a few moments, which helps brighten the taste a bit, dry them again, and then cover them in olive oil. Use them within the week. See the Resources section (page 225) for where to find them online, or buy them in an Italian grocery.

Tomato paste

Use Sicilian strattu. There isn't any commercially available tomato paste that's better. Good strattu (or estratto) and tomato paste are barely even the same product. Strattu is a deep, brick-red color and has a claylike consistency that is so thick you can cut it with a knife. It is traditionally made from hand-selected, top-quality plum tomatoes that are skinned, seeded, pureed, salted, and cooked down a little before being spread on wooden trays to dry slowly in the sun over a period of several days. Tomato paste is still made in a similar fashion in parts of North Africa, Turkey, and the Middle East, but with different varieties of tomatoes. You should be able to find a good version from the Italian importers I list in the Resources section (page 225).

Olive oil

I generally only buy Italian olive oil. Our friends at Gustiamo, an Italian food importer, wrote a primer on how to tell the real deal. Here's the gist:

ESSENTIAL INGREDIENTS

1) The label should say "Italian Olive Oil" or "Olio Extra Vergine di Oliva Italiano," not "Product of Italy." When it says the latter, it does not mean that the actual oil is made with Italian olives or that the olives were milled in Italy. It means it was bottled in Italy. That label allows for the mixing of olives from different countries and different levels of freshness (or rancidity).
2) It should have a harvest date that indicates freshness. Otherwise, the oil might be a mixture of olive oils coming from different countries, or oil made with olives harvested in different years, or both.
3) When it comes to extra virgin, cold-pressed and filtered olive oil: it doesn't mean that the oil is fresh or milled and stored properly.

Because there are so few regulations in terms of olive oil, I cannot tell you what label to look for or how, exactly, to buy it. Here's what I can tell you. People have become more aware of slave labor in fishing and other industries, but workers in the olive oil industry suffer much like slave labor on fishing boats. You can avoid supporting unjust work practices by ensuring that your olive oil is made by a small family business that owns both their trees and their mill. Owning both is important for traceability and purity. Yes, it is more expensive. But if you buy a few better ingredients rather than many cheaper ingredients, your food will taste better and be healthier for everyone.

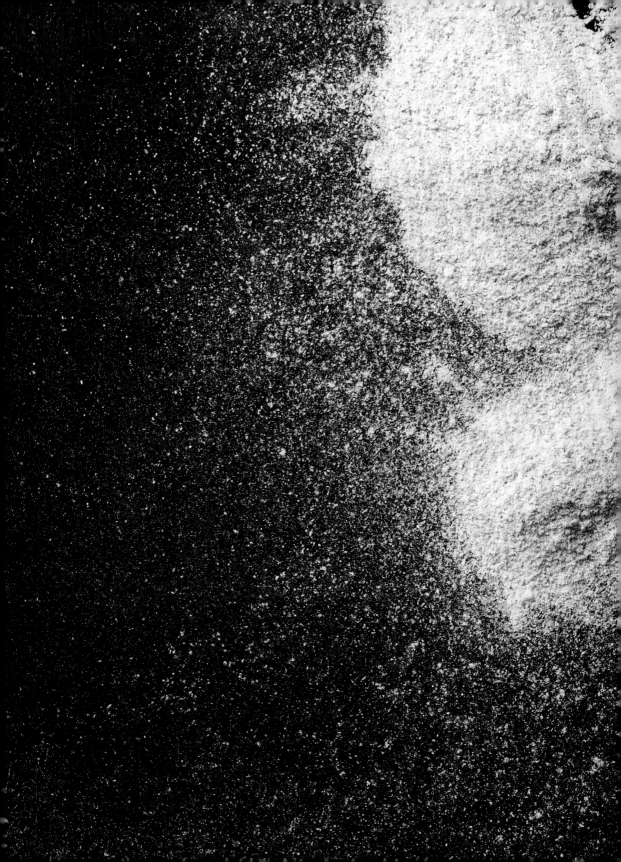

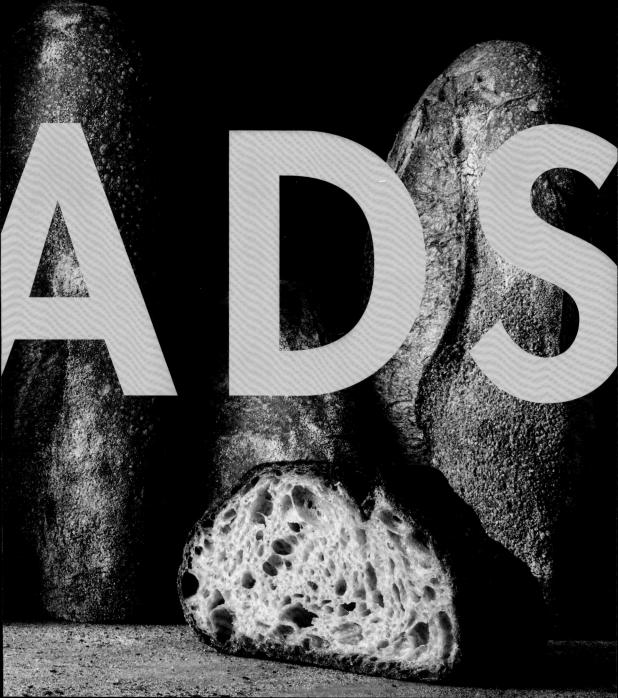

This is not intended to be a baking book. I had originally planned to not have any bread recipes at all. Having started as a home baker myself, I think home baking is unnecessarily difficult and incredibly inefficient. But no publisher wants to touch a book about bread without bread recipes in it, so I've provided a few. I'm not trying to present signature breads here—many great books have already been written on the topic. Still, while I don't provide very much to build on what's already out there, I've offered some basic ideas to help you further understand the process of baking and what it involves.

One more note: I've kept the bread recipes in grams as opposed to standard measurement because it's more precise and I think many bakers before me have made the case of why metric measurement is so important in bread baking. Outside of the baking chapter, I have both grams and standard measurement since those recipes are more flexible and in part so you can keep the ratios that I'm suggesting.

STARTER

When it comes to baking bread, sure, you can follow my recipe or anyone else's. The recipe is beside the point. What has value is that you learn your starter. You learn how to care for it. You learn the discipline and the rigidity it requires to get it on a predictable schedule. You learn what it needs and how to take care of those needs.

Your starter will become stronger the more you feed it over time. Using the method below, the starter will be ready in seven to ten days, but it might not be very consistent or predictable until you have fed it for a longer period of time. Your second or third loaf made with this starter will likely turn out better than the first—because your starter will be healthier and more stable by then.

I do not suggest refrigerating your starter at any point, especially when you're trying to establish it—otherwise, the yeast will get too sluggish. In fact, I don't recommend refrigerating it ever. But if you have to—you're going to be away for an extended period of time and you want to retard the growth—wait until it has at least tripled in size (after several days) before you do. (See below for exact directions on refrigerating.)

Instructions

Note: The key here is temperature. Yeasts favor a temperature from 78° to 82°F; 80°–82°F is optimal. You'll need to set up a place in your house that will allow you to keep the starter at that temperature. (There are all kinds of ways you can do this: inside your oven with the light on, for example, or in your microwave.) It is important to invest in both room and probe thermometers to make sure the right temperature is maintained at all times.

To make the starter: Place the raisins in the container, along with 200 grams of spring water heated to 78°–80°F. Keep the mixture loosely covered with the dish towel for 24 hours, kept between the high 70s and 80°F. Generally, once you have made bread with the starter a few times, you will be able to use tap water. But when you're →

WHAT YOU'LL NEED

A kitchen scale

A clean, clear container that can hold up to 4 cups of liquid

A clean dish towel

A space that maintains 78°–82°F (see note below)

A room thermometer that's more exact than a thermostat or probe thermometer

INGREDIENTS

50 grams raisins

1500–2000 grams spring water (100 grams per 15–20 feedings, plus an additional 100 grams per feeding)

100 grams stone-milled rye flour or stone-milled whole-wheat flour

1500–2000 grams strong white bread flour—at least 12 percent protein (100 grams per 15–20 feedings)

getting a new culture established, you don't want to introduce anything that's going to make it harder to establish a culture, such as fluoride or chlorine.

After 24 hours, strain out and discard the raisins, reserving the liquid. Mix 100 grams of that infused water with the stone-milled rye flour or stone-milled whole-wheat flour. (Rye tends to be a little more active and makes the process go faster.) Keep that mixture covered loosely with a clean dish towel for 24 to 72 hours at 78°–80°F.

During that time, you should notice a slight increase in volume and some bubbles in the mass. This means it's ready for the next step; it can happen in as little as 24 hours and as long as 72. (The last time I did it, it was ready in 36 hours.)

If the mass does nothing within 72 hours, throw it away and start over.

After you've seen the slight increase in volume and bubbles on the surface, scrape off the surface if it's dry. Mix 100 grams of the remaining liquid with 100 grams of white bread flour and 100 grams of 80°F spring water. Put this mixture back in the 78°–80°F spot for another 24 hours. At this point you should be able to detect real activity, as it rises. Once every 24 hours, feed it with 100 grams of bread flour and 100 grams of spring water, stirring it gently with a spoon or your clean fingers to mix, as long as it's rising and has activity.

After the third day, if the starter is rising consistently, feed it at shorter intervals: every 12 hours for two successive feedings. What you're looking for is the starter to triple in volume. It should be active and frothy.

Your goal is to train your starter to reach that peak within 3 or 4 hours. After the two 12-hour feedings, you should feed it every 8 hours until you get to a point that you're feeding it every 3 to 4 hours. At that point, you can begin using it to make bread. It's not about the time it takes; your starter will have more than tripled in volume, so you'll have to feed it more frequently.

If you plan to use the starter soon (or daily), keep it at that warm temperature and feed it two or three times a week. If you are going to use it later, cover and store the remaining starter in the refrigerator, feeding it once a week. To reactivate it, return it to the 78°–82°F environment and feed it two or three times before you use it.

I have lost so much of my zealotry when it comes to flour. I think it's fine to use white flour. I think it's fine to use yeast in certain cases to get certain results. A good baker has developed sensitivity through the process of baking, and then can know what went wrong and know how to correct mistakes. You don't get that from a recipe. You don't get that from a book. You get that from making bread badly again and again and again and again— and by paying attention to the process and the results.

BREAD FOR HOME BAKERS

Makes 2 loaves

As I have expressed, I am not the biggest fan of home baking. But I've done enough of it to be able to offer some pointers and direction if you want to pursue it and it brings you pleasure and joy—or if you are just interested in better understanding the basic mechanics of bread making. If you are looking for tricks to make great bread at home, those books have been written and I don't have much to add to the subject.

To begin with, all flours are different, sometimes even from batch to batch from the same mill. Certainly, it is different from mill to mill, especially if you are sourcing flour from small local producers. I can offer a set of basic parameters and tell you to find flour with a certain protein level—but be careful. Protein percentages only paint a partial picture and don't really give any indication of gluten quality; some of my favorite breads I have made were with flours that had only 9 or 10 percent protein, and I have made plenty of terrible bread with flours coming in at 13 to 14 percent protein.

I can also tell you to make sure that the "falling number" of the wheat used to mill the flour is above 300. The falling number indicates the level of enzymatic activity. The lower the number, the higher the enzymatic activity, which indicates sprouting damage to the wheat and lower-quality flour. This is a more common problem for wheat producers in wetter parts of the country and generally a good thing to know.

But these are just numbers and technical details, and they can't take the place of forming your own relationship with the flour and, by extension, a miller. Great bakers rely on a lot of sensory cues that can help them make adjustments in the process as necessary.

One difficulty in bread recipes is that your starter will be different from mine. Even if I gave you some of my own, the yeast populations and various microflora in your home would change the starter over time. In addition to forming a relationship with flour, you need to develop a relationship with your starter. You should understand its cycles, rhythms, and behavior, keep it on a consistent feeding schedule, and learn to understand what it needs, when it needs it, and how it performs best.

Environment is another huge factor. Commercial bakeries have large proofers and temperature-controlled rooms to keep the fermentation and maturation of the dough on a predictable schedule. People suggest all manner of workarounds to create some semblance of temperature control for the home baker. You could put the bread in the oven with the light on and the temperature off. Maybe your pilot light will be enough to provide consistent warmth. An electric aquarium heater in a cooler with some rigged-up control system might work. Or you could place a space heater in a closet and set it on very low, or buy a small proofer designed for home bakers. All of this seems impractical and expensive to me, and it's a lot of effort. But if you are thoroughly committed and handy—go for it: rig something up.

Part of the problem here, however, is the mass effect. A large amount of dough holds its temperature for a much longer period. As a result, it tends to ferment more thoroughly and evenly than smaller amounts, which will quickly equalize to room temperature. Since it is impractical to make large amounts of dough in a home setting, I suggest just going with the ambient conditions and adapting your process to them.

Consistency in temperature helps you predict a general time line for your bread. Since the actual temperature of the room is often different from the setting on your house thermostat, you should invest in some room thermometers so you can keep accurate track.

If, as an example, we assume that the room where you are storing your flour and baking is between 68° and 76°F, I would suggest using water right around the same temperature and adjusting the amount of starter used in your bread: If the air is closer to 68°F, I recommend using 5–6 percent (relative to the amount of flour) active starter when you mix your bread and decreasing that number as the temperature increases. →

If the temperature drops or increases outside of that range, use cooler or warmer water to adjust the temperature of your dough. The goal is to have the temperature of the dough match the surrounding air.

If you want to learn to make bread, and especially if you want to make good bread, the best advice I can give is to make a lot of bad bread. And I mean *a lot*. I still do it pretty often myself. It isn't a fast method, but it is the best way to figure out what things are supposed to look like, feel like, smell like, and taste like at every step in the process.

To even start down that path, you have to develop a clear idea of what you define as good bread. Understand what you are trying to attain and then figure out how to get there.

This recipe is not for beginners. If it's your first time baking bread, I suggest you try the excellent no-knead recipe from Jim Lahey, widely available online. Try it with a bunch of different flours—particularly some you might order from, say, Community Grains (see Resources on page 225), or others that you pick up at a farmers market. Try that recipe with a blend of whole-wheat and white flours. And then move on to the more involved recipe from Chad Robertson's book *Tartine* and do the same thing. Slight variations in temperature, humidity, and the flour you're using will make a difference in timing and the performance of the dough.

This is how I bake bread. And it truly can vary according to the weather—or even whether my oven has been on all day and makes the room hotter. I'm not going to simplify it for you: I want to emphasize here that you are not making an industrialized product with mass-produced ingredients. Bread baking is like taking care of a child—or at the very least a small pet. You have to be committed and pay attention to details. And you have to be okay with the fact that details are going to vary. The only way they're not is if you use a simplified or dumbed-down recipe, commercial yeast, and mass-produced ingredients.

That said, mine is a lot like other bread recipes that require starters. I'm not reinventing the wheel here.

Instructions

Note: The temperature of your water is crucial. Calculate the correct temperature by determining the temperature of your room and the temperature of your starter. You want a final dough temperature of about 78°F. Multiply 78 by 4, which gives you a base temperature of 312°F. Subtract the temperature of the flour and the temperature of the starter. The number you arrive at should give you a good ballpark of what your water temperature should be. Friction is negligible when you're mixing by hand. An accurate thermometer is essential.

A kitchen scale

A digital thermometer

A straight-sided, lightly oiled container, preferably with a lid, where your dough will rise

One or two Dutch ovens

A bench (dough) scraper

Two proofing baskets (or two dish towels in two bowls or colanders)

INGREDIENTS

800 grams water (or more; see instructions)

1000 grams bread flour, plus more for the counter

200 grams Starter (fully ripe; see page 3)

25 grams salt

Mix 700 grams of the water with all of the flour in a mixing bowl large enough to hold everything with some room, until no dry flour remains. Cover the bowl with plastic wrap and transfer to a warm place (78°–82°F) to rest for 20 minutes or so. After this period of rest, mix in your starter with a splash of the remaining water. Use your fingers to work everything into a homogeneous mass. Cover and let rest for another 10 minutes or so, back in that warm place. At this point, mix in the salt with an additional splash of the reserved water until completely dissolved. Rest, covered, back in the warm spot, for another 15 minutes.

After 15 minutes, grab a corner of the dough, stretch it out, and fold it into the center of the mass. Repeat this, rotating the bowl until the dough feels taut and gives resistance. Flip the dough over, leaving the smooth side up, cover, and rest in the warm space for another 15 minutes.

At this point, the dough should be building strength, getting smoother and stronger, depending on your choice of flour. It may need more water. Add it gradually and see how it does. You will learn to feel and read the capabilities of different flours as you continue to work with them.

After the three foldings with 15 minutes in between, transfer the dough to the straight-sided, lightly oiled container. Mark the side of the container with a piece of tape to indicate where the top of the dough is.

A half hour after this series of folds, fold again. This time, you want to wet the counter a little (damp, not a puddle). →

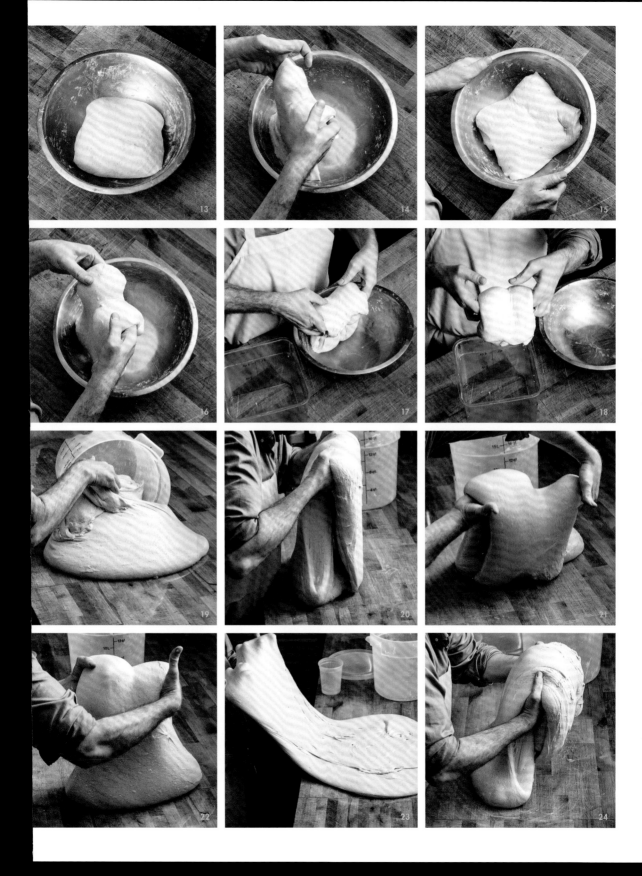

Pour out the dough and fold by picking up the dough underneath itself. (The photos on pages 12 and 13 illustrate this better than I can explain.) Place the dough back in the container, smooth side up, and keep in the warm place.

Repeat this folding every half hour, being progressively more gentle as the dough gains strength and begins to trap more air. Once the dough begins to become strong and gassy, stop folding and just let it rise. The folds, or proofing, should take 4 to 6 hours, depending on temperature, the health of your starter, and the strength of your flour. When the dough has risen one-third to one-half of its original volume, it is time to divide and shape.

To check whether the dough is ready, you can pinch off a corner and put it in water to see whether it floats. If you're having trouble telling whether your dough has risen enough to shape, this is a good test.

Once the dough is ready, lightly flour your counter. Pour out the mass of dough there. Use a bench scraper to cut the mass in half. (Note: The smaller amount of dough you have, the harder it is to hold its temperature—that's why a 5000-gram mass of dough is going to ferment much more thoroughly than a 500-gram mass of dough, and why you often have enough dough for two loaves in this and other recipes.)

Depending on how much your dough has risen, you will need to shape each loaf with more or less tension. If your dough hasn't risen very much and it's on the younger side of development, you can give it a "pre-shape." Take your bench scraper and use it to round the dough from the underneath, flour side up, using the surface of your counter to help create tension. Then let the dough rest for 20 minutes or, if your kitchen is cold, up to 1 hour.

(I don't normally waste time with pre-shaping. When working with larger amounts of dough, part of the benefits of pre-shaping include slowing down fermentation, adding a little strength if the dough is very slack, and creating a more symmetrical form to make final shaping easier. Pre-shaping also helps if you are scaling your dough to a precise weight and aren't great at it. If there are a lot of small pieces in your dough, the period of bench rest after you pre-shape helps them to incorporate. I prefer to do a longer bulk fermentation and get a little more gas and air into the dough and then shape it in a kind of looser, simpler fashion.)

If you are not pre-shaping, the next step is to take your bench scraper and make sure the two pieces of dough aren't stuck to the counter. You want to gently get your hands underneath one portion of dough, fold the two sides in toward the middle, then use your fingertips to reach under and fold the dough on top of itself. Flip down the top lobe to create a little bit of a roll, then use your fingers—not just your fingertips. Extend your thumbs and use them to roll up the entire mass, creating surface tension. Think of this technique like rolling up a little sleeping bag.

In this process, you have to make sure that you don't have any loose flour inside the dough and that the floured part of the dough always remains on the outside. You also want to make sure that there isn't any flour in the seam when you roll up the dough; otherwise, it won't seal. Shape the second portion of dough in the same fashion.

Then, use your bench scraper and your hand as guides to pick up each loaf and drop them into separate floured proofing baskets, seam side down.

At this point, you can put the doughs in their proofing baskets back in the warm place and allow them to rise anywhere from 2 to 4 hours. But don't watch the clock, watch the dough. You're looking for them to increase one and a half times in volume. They should look light and pillowy, and spring back very, very slowly when pressed with a fingertip.

If you don't have that much time, you can put them in a warm place for about an hour, then place them in your refrigerator overnight. But generally speaking, I don't like the refrigerator for making doughs with a starter because they tend to move too slowly at 41°F or less. Most home refrigerators are too cold. Commercial yeast pushes through at cold temperatures, but these doughs almost →

stop altogether. Alternatively, if you have a place that's 50°F, they will continue to grow overnight.

An hour before you bake the breads—whether it's that day, or the next—you want to preheat your Dutch oven(s), with the lids on, for an hour at 500°F. You can bake two breads simultaneously; if you have just one Dutch oven, the second proofed loaf can sit and wait (see below).

You may then want to put a small piece of parchment on the inside bottom of each Dutch oven to keep the breads from burning, especially if you're using a conventional as opposed to a convection oven. Dump each proofed loaf into its own heated Dutch oven—seam side up, so you don't have to score the loaves—using oven mitts or towels so you don't burn yourself. Put the lids on and return the loaves to the oven.

A few minutes in, reduce the temperature to 460°F. Allow the loaves to bake, covered, for 20 minutes. Then take off the lids and bake for about 40 minutes, or until the crusts achieve your desired color. (I like mine somewhere between caramel and mahogany.)

Remove the loaves and set them to cool on a rack so they have air circulation.

Don't eat too much hot bread, or it'll give you a stomachache.

If you are working with a single Dutch oven, return it to the oven and increase the temperature to 500°F. After about 30 minutes, remove it from the oven, place a new piece of parchment in the pot, and repeat the baking process (lid on, reduced temperature with lid off after 20 minutes, etc.).

FRISELLE

Makes about 32 friselle, after splitting and baking

Friselle (frisella, singular) are far too underappreciated in the United States. In the general category of rusks, they are a southern Italian staple with roots in antiquity. These are breads designed for long-term storage; when made correctly they should be dry and hard and never go bad.

Though they are most commonly associated with Puglia, friselle are also widely found and enjoyed in Lazio, Campania, Calabria, and Basilicata. In all likelihood, they originated in Greece, where they are still eaten widely and known as paximadia. Friselle can be made in a variety of shapes and styles and are often made with different flours. Feel free to experiment with durum wheat, white flour, rye, spelt, and other grains. My favorite types of friselle are made with whole wheat or a blend of whole wheat and barley. Traditionally and more efficiently, friselle were, and in some places still are, made with the same dough used to make bread. As the fashion has shifted to breads made with softer, wetter doughs, it is better (but less efficient) to make them with a dedicated, stiffer dough.

Friselle can be eaten in a number of ways. You can rub the rough side of a dry frisella with a clove of garlic before briefly rehydrating it with a dip in cold water (or even a quick trip under the faucet). At this point, you can sprinkle on a little dried oregano, a pinch of salt, and a drizzle of oil and eat as is for a simple and austere snack. Or top with quartered or halved cherry tomatoes, fresh basil or oregano, oil, and salt. You can dress them up with capers or olives, a little hot pepper, and oil-packed tuna or an anchovy or two. Or mozzarella. The options are almost limitless. Alternatively, you can grate a ripe tomato onto the rough side of the frisella like a Spanish pan con tomate, and season as you like.

You can also break the dry friselle into pieces and put them in a tomato salad or other salad to soften in the juices and make a sort of panzanella. But friselle shouldn't be limited to the summer months. They are great broken into soups, especially with any kinds of beans or →

legumes, or placed in the bottom of a bowl of clams or a seafood stew of some sort. Even in times when you don't have any bread in the house, you can always have friselle. Feel free to double or triple this recipe so you can build up your supply.

Just a note: This takes about two days from start to finish, so clear your schedule.

Instructions

Mix 650 grams (about 2¾ cups) of the water with the flour in a mixing bowl, working it by hand until no dry flour remains. This may take some effort, as this is a stiff dough.

Cover the dough with a lid and allow it to rest at room temperature for at least 1 hour, and up to 2 hours. Give the dough a series of folds every half hour during the 2 hours, and then again if it seems slack.

Once the dough has rested and your starter is ready, mix in your starter by hand. When it is well incorporated, mix in the salt with a little bit of the remaining water; you may not need all of it.

Knead the dough on a clean, lightly floured work surface for at least 10 minutes, or until it is completely smooth and strong, adding any of the remaining water as needed if the dough feels impossibly stiff or dry. You do not want a wet dough.

Place in a straight-sided, lightly oiled container in a cool place (68°–70°F). Use a piece of tape to mark the height of the dough on the outside of your container so you can clearly monitor the growth.

After 1 to 2 hours, once the dough has risen by one-third to one-half more than its original volume (which should take about 16 hours), dump it out onto a lightly floured counter and divide into 16 pieces that each weigh about 150 grams. Shape each one into a ball and allow them to rest for 20 to 30 minutes, or potentially longer if it is →

INGREDIENTS

700 grams cool water, or as needed

1000 grams stone-milled whole-wheat flour, plus more for shaping

60 grams Starter (see page 3)

25 grams salt

Oil for proofing

cool in the room or the first rise of the dough was closer to a third larger than a half.

Once the balls of dough have relaxed a little, lightly re-flour the counter and place a dough ball on it. Flour the top of the dough ball, then poke your finger through the center to make a hole. Stretch the hole a little wider, either on the table or using both of your hands until you have what looks like a doughnut that is 4 or 5 inches wide. Gently flatten the doughnut, and place on a floured linen or wooden board. Repeat the process with the remaining balls of dough.

Allow the dough balls to rise in a slightly warmer place until they have increased one and a half times their original volume and spring back slowly when indented with a finger; this will take a couple of hours.

Preheat your oven to 425°F.

Once the dough is ready, place on a baking sheet lined with parchment paper and bake for 20 minutes. Remove from the oven, and, while still warm, split the friselle with a wire or a knife. (I use one of the spokes on Metro shelving.) Cutting the friselle with a knife creates a much smoother surface, which is not as desirable, but do what works for you.

Line several more baking sheets with parchment paper. Reduce the oven temperature to 300°F. Place the friselle, split sides up, on the sheets and bake until they have completely dried out, rotating as necessary to prevent them from darkening too much. This should take about an hour. The friselle should have no give when pressed with a finger. When they are completely cool, store friselle in an airtight container. If they are totally dry, they will keep indefinitely.

PIZZA BIANCA

Makes two 13 x 18 sheet pans

25

INGREDIENTS

720 grams strong bread flour, plus more for the counter

80 grams semola rimacinata or "extra fancy" durum wheat flour

6 grams fresh yeast or 2 grams instant dry yeast

600 grams cold water, plus another 40 grams to help dissolve the salt, and more for your hands and counter

20 grams salt

24 grams olive oil, plus more for the pan, the surface of the dough, and topping

Salt for topping the dough

Pizza bianca Romana, sometimes referred to as focaccia Romana, as we know it today is a relatively modern bakery product that evolved with developments in bakery technology like spiral mixers, precision electric deck ovens, and temperature control. It is pretty hard to replicate these at home, although it's maybe a little easier than other styles of pizza that rely on the intense heat of a wood-burning oven. It can be used like a pizza, with toppings (see pages 29–30), or as bread, which is how I use it in many of the recipes in this book.

This recipe and method isn't what I use at my shop, but the basic principles are solid and will help you understand something of the process. This recipe and ideas owe an enormous debt to Gabriele Bonci, although this isn't what he does, either. If you are a pizza person and want to learn more about it, buy his book.

A couple of suggestions: Use the shittiest, flimsiest cookie sheets or baking pans you can find; generally, these conduct heat a little better than fancier ones. Traditionally, professionals use thin carbon steel or blue steel pans, but they can be expensive and I would suggest using what you already have and getting better at making pizza before making the investment.

A note on semola rimacinata: In Italy, durum wheat is milled into varying levels of coarseness or fineness depending on its intended use and the characteristics of the wheat. To keep things simple, there is semola and semola rimacinata (or "reground"), which is finer. In the United States, the closest thing we have is often sold with the designation "extra fancy." It is usually finer than semola rimacinata, but it will work great here. You do not want semolina, which is much coarser.

Instructions

Mix the flours in a large bowl. Add the yeast and 600 grams of cold water. In the heat of summer, use ice to get the →

water cold (but strain out the ice before mixing the water with the flour). In the winter, cold tap water should be fine.

Mix by hand until no dry flour remains and the yeast is fully incorporated.

Cover the bowl with plastic wrap or a clean towel and let it rest for 15 minutes.

Add the salt and the 40 grams of water to help dissolve the salt, and mix by hand until fully incorporated into the dough.

Cover the bowl and allow the dough to rest for 10 minutes.

Wet your hands so the dough doesn't stick to them and give the dough a series of folds (pages 12 and 13). in the bowl, place the smooth side up, and cover. Wait another 10 minutes. Repeat this process two more times.

After the third series of folds, use the 24 grams of olive oil to liberally oil a medium-sized straight-sided container. Place the dough in the container and pour any remaining olive oil on top. It will eventually be absorbed into the dough. Use a piece of tape to mark the level of the dough in the container to help you judge the rise. Place a lid on the container of dough and put it in the refrigerator.

An hour later, remove the container. Wet a clean space on the counter, pour out the dough, and fold it to build more tension. Place it back in the container and put it back in the refrigerator.

Go on with your life. If you think of it when you pass the refrigerator in the course of your day, or at least before you go to bed that night, check the dough. If it looks slack and flat in the container, take it out and give it another series of folds on the counter before placing it back into the container and the refrigerator.

Early in the process, lots of folding is good. You want to build enough strength in the dough so it can withstand a long fermentation. As the dough begins to rise and develop air bubbles, you'll want to fold it less and more gently when you do.

The following day, check your dough. Give it another series of folds and place back into the refrigerator. →

The dough should double in size within two to three days depending on the temperature of your refrigerator. If it doesn't or you want to use it earlier, take it out of the refrigerator and let it sit on the counter in a warm place in your kitchen until it doubles in size or at least gets to one and a half times its original volume before you proceed to the next step.

Once it's about double the size, pour out the dough onto a lightly floured counter and cut in half.

Gently roll each mass of dough as you would making a loaf of bread and place seam side down on a lightly oiled pan. Lightly oil the surface of the dough and cover with plastic wrap to prevent a skin from forming and place in a warm place to rise.

Preheat the oven to the maximum temperature with a pizza stone on the lowest rung of the oven for at least an hour. When the dough has again doubled in size (4 to 6 hours depending on temperature—watch the dough, not the clock), gently stretch it and press it out to fill the pan, dimpling it with the pads of your fingers, paying special attention to the edges to make sure they don't puff up too much in the oven. You don't really want to knock the air out of the dough here, but you do want to redistribute it relatively evenly.

Drizzle with olive oil and a give it a light sprinkle of salt. Place in the hot oven on the pizza stone and bake for 15 to 20 minutes, until it is golden and crisp. If the bottom is coloring too quickly, move it up to a higher rack in the oven to finish.

Pizzas

While I often use pizza bianca as bread, it can, of course, also be used to make pizza.

It bothers me that Americans—maybe everyone—revert to their six-year-old selves when it comes to pizza, seemingly losing all critical faculties, and sometimes their manners. Maybe because pizza is traditionally a street food. Maybe because it's often slathered in cheese. But good pizza really is all about the bread—and that's something our culture doesn't really acknowledge. Here are a few to get you started. →

PIZZA WITH PEPPERS (AND SOME VARIATIONS)

The following recipe for pizza with peppers is as good as any place to start and it's the one that Mark Bittman included in his last column for *The New York Times* about my bakery. Following this recipe, I have riffs that include the classic rosso, margherita, pizza with fried eggplant, and pizza with pureed squash and sage. Feel free to come up with your own variations. But generally, season and prepare your toppings in advance before dressing the pizza.

INGREDIENTS

5 bell peppers

2 tablespoons (about 30 grams) olive oil (page xxxi) plus more for the pan and for drizzling

½ teaspoon salt

One recipe pizza bianca dough (page 25)

Flour, for dusting

8 ounces (about 225–230 grams) fresh mozzarella, torn into small pieces

1 tablespoon chopped fresh rosemary leaves

Instructions

If you have a pizza stone, slide it onto the lowest rack or on the floor of your oven, and heat the oven to 500°F. Heat for at least 30 minutes and preferably longer before baking.

Slice the bell peppers thinly, discarding the seedy cores. Sauté, stirring frequently, over medium heat with 2 tablespoons of extra-virgin olive oil and salt until tender, 15 to 20 minutes.

Lightly grease an 18 x 13 inch pan with olive oil. Wipe the pan clean with a dry paper towel; it's important not to bake the pizza on too much oil. Flip out the dough onto a floured surface and gently press out into a rectangle ½ to ¾ inch thick, being careful not to deflate the dough too much. Place one forearm over the dough, and use the other hand to flip the dough over your forearm and into the pan, leaving the floured side up. Rearrange the dough on the pan, again pressing only lightly.

Spread the toppings (sauteed peppers, mozzarella, rosemary, black pepper) evenly across the dough, drizzle generously with oil, and bake on the pizza stone (or directly on the bottom of the oven or lowest rack) for 5 minutes. Move the pizza to the middle rack in the →

oven, and continue to bake for 10 to 15 more minutes, or until golden brown.

Using a bench scraper or metal spatula, scoop under the pizza, and scrape to release it from the pan. This may take some blind faith and a bit of elbow grease. Slide out onto a cutting board and slice into pieces using a chef's knife, kitchen scissors, or a pizza cutter. Serve immediately or at room temperature, or reheat.

Variations

Rosso: Drain and crush high-quality canned tomatoes and bake with those, dried Italian oregano, olive oil, and salt.

Margherita: Drain and crush high-quality canned tomatoes and bake with those, mozzarella, basil, olive oil, and salt.

Fried eggplant: Drain and crush high-quality canned tomatoes and bake, then top with breaded fried eggplant (page 148) and cherry tomato salad with croutons (page 92).

Squash: Bake with roasted winter squash puree, then top with sage, olive oil, a light squeeze of lemon juice, and salt.

Keep it *plain* and use it for sandwiches (see page 57).

Slice your bread as you go. I promise, you'll be glad you do. We Americans usually insist on buying our bread sliced, but we shouldn't. It ensures that our bread will go stale sooner. Our bread also usually comes in a crappy plastic bag, which traps in moisture and makes bread get moldy, negating the purpose of the crust, which protects your bread and makes it last longer.

Coming up, we've got some toasts that are well out of the realm of the avocado repertoire and in some cases may even be new to you. I've also included a bunch of variations. While I tend to feel strongly about most things when it comes to food, I really have a lot to say about sandwiches, since a good sandwich is hard to find.

RICOTTA AND HONEY

Serves 1

This is something of a non-recipe, but it is a significant one to me.

When I first opened Bread and Salt in Pittsburgh, it blew my mind that I had trouble selling people a one-kilo loaf of naturally leavened bread made entirely of organic heirloom wheat for $11, but I could take those same loaves of bread I couldn't sell the day before, cut them into thick slices, toast them, put something on top, and sell each slice for $6 faster than I could assemble them.

Toast was having a moment, and I loathed that moment. My taste for toast—specifically this toast, with ricotta and honey—led to the first significant national press the bakery received, in *T: The New York Times Style Magazine*. Immediately afterward, it seemed as if everyone who came through the door wanted ricotta and honey toast no matter what else was on the menu. Toast with cultured butter and bottarga? No. Stracciatella with blood orange and mint? Nope. Wild serviceberry jam? Forget it. Ricotta and honey toast. Always. I grew to despise it—except that ricotta and honey make a classic, almost magical combination that tastes incredible. I still make it for myself for breakfast when I have great ricotta on hand.

My favorite honey for this is dark, almost medicinal, with a slightly bitter edge. I typically use a locally produced buckwheat honey.

INGREDIENTS

Olive oil

Thick slice of naturally leavened white bread (1–3 days old; see headnote)

Top-quality fresh ricotta

Salt

Coarsely ground black pepper

Dark honey, such as buckwheat

Instructions

Heat a skillet over medium heat. Drizzle in some olive oil, then add one slice of bread. Place a bacon press or something similar on top of it to make sure the underside is completely in contact with the pan. Toast as you like it, turning it over just once. Transfer to a plate.

Spoon a generous dollop of ricotta on the top side of the toast. Lightly season with salt and pepper. Drizzle with dark honey.

So, let's talk about ricotta.

Ricotta means "recooked," and it is made from the whey left over from the process of making other cheese. True ricotta has an incredibly clean, milky taste. The best versions allow you a slight taste of what the animals themselves have been eating and change with the seasons depending on the grasses growing at the time. The texture of top-quality fresh ricotta is light and soft—never rubbery or, even worse, chewy.

The majority of ricotta sold in the United States is not good. What is sold in U.S. stores as whole-milk or part-skim ricotta is essentially acidified curdled milk, drained and packed in containers often with added stabilizers or preservatives. At the other end of the spectrum there is ricotta di pecora, crafted by cheesemakers in southern Italy, preferably bought when it is fresh and still warm. Now that would make some fine ricotta and honey toast.

Alternatively, and perhaps more realistically, seek out ricotta made by cheesemakers where you live (cow's-, sheep's- or goat's-milk ricotta can all be lovely). Ask about how they make it. If you cannot find any ricotta made in the traditional manner, don't bother with this toast; make something else.

FRENCH TOAST

Serves any number

In France, French toast is known as "pain perdu"—lost bread. The idea is that soaking stale bread in beaten eggs and milk is a way to make it edible again and save it from being thrown away. Recipes along the same lines have a precedent in the ancient world and are mentioned as early as the fourth or fifth century in *Apicius*, the famous collection of really old recipes from Rome.

I've always kind of disliked French toast because it is so often mushy. Using very stale bread solves this problem and therefore makes the best French toast. The drier the bread, the more it can absorb without losing all of its texture.

Making good French toast requires a little planning. If I know I will be preparing this sometime during the week, I cut one-and-a-half-inch slices of a rustic loaf (say, two slices per person) at least two to three days ahead of time. If it's good bread—naturally leavened, high-hydration, the whole nine yards—starting with a loaf that is two or three days old is fine. (If it is much older than that, it can be hard to slice, even with a great bread knife.) It also requires an overnight soak in the refrigerator, so plan accordingly.

I let the slices sit on the counter or my breadboard. If you are worried about pests, you can place the slices in a cupboard or in another dry, enclosed space. Once a day, check the progress of your bread as it dries out and hardens. Turn it over. Sit it upright on its bottom crust, its crumb exposed for maximum air circulation.

INGREDIENTS

2 slices dried rustic bread per serving, 1½ inches thick (see above)

1 egg per slice

½ cup milk (or ¼ cup milk plus ¼ cup heavy cream/120 ml in total) per slice

Pinch of salt

Pinch of sugar, a splash of vanilla extract or orange blossom water, or a drizzle of honey (for sweet French toast, optional)

Unsalted butter for the pan

Pats of salted butter, or warm honey, jam, or maple syrup for serving

Instructions

Arrange the dried bread in a single layer in a shallow baking dish that is just large enough to snugly hold the number of slices you are using, so all the eggs and milk will be absorbed.

Crack 1 egg for each slice into a mixing bowl and beat thoroughly, then whisk in ½ cup of the dairy for each →

egg. Add a small pinch of salt, and, for sweet French toast, a pinch of sugar, a splash of vanilla or orange blossom water, or a drizzle of honey.

Pour the egg-milk mixture over the bread, which will not be completely submerged; that is okay. Turn the slices over to coat evenly. Cover with plastic wrap and refrigerate for 8 to 12 hours, or overnight, turning the slices over at least once after a few hours. You want the bread to absorb as much of the liquid as possible. It should be soft but not falling apart.

Over medium heat, heat a skillet (or a griddle) large enough to allow the slices of soaked bread full contact with its surface. Toss in a knob of unsalted butter and let it melt until the foaming subsides. Carefully place a slice or two of soaked bread in the pan and reduce the heat to medium. Pour any unabsorbed egg-milk mixture over the slices in the pan, being careful not to spill any into the pan itself.

Cook for a few minutes, then lift a corner of one of the slices to check on the browning. (I like it to be a nice golden brown, but not too dark because overcooked eggs taste terrible.) If the color is where it should be, turn the slices to brown on the other side. Monitor the heat, adjusting it as needed. You want the surfaces of the French toast to be nicely browned and the interior just set. You can also place the pan (assuming it is ovenproof) in a 375°F oven immediately after you turn the toast if you are concerned about it burning over direct heat. Repeat as needed, depending on how many pieces of French toast you are cooking.

Serve as is, or top with salted butter and warm honey, jam, or maple syrup.

BREAD, BUTTER, AND ANCHOVIES

This is a classic and prevalent combination and a great appetizer, snack, part of a meal, and so on. Go with the best butter you have—something cultured and salted. With fresh bread, I recommend using soft, room-temperature butter. If your bread is a few days old, toast it first. Slice cold butter—as much as you like—and place it on top of the bread so it doesn't all melt into the face of the warm toast. Then top it with one or two or even three cleaned anchovy fillets (see page xxxi) depending on the size of the piece of bread, the salt content of your butter, and your appetite. A little black pepper or lemon zest can be nice here but is not really necessary.

BREAD, BUTTER, AND BOTTARGA

This is the same idea as the previous recipe. The contrast of the salty, briny fish against the rich creamy taste of the butter with the bread to bring it all together and convey it to your mouth is what works here. Bottarga is the salted, cured, pressed roe sac of a grey mullet or a tuna. The production of bottarga is widely spread throughout the Mediterranean (and more recently Florida) and reaches far back into antiquity. Peel off any coating your piece of bottarga might have, then grate or shave the roe extremely thinly onto your buttered bread or toast. A drop of lemon juice and a touch of zest can lift up the taste a little.

BREAD AND CHOCOLATE

This seems too simple to put in print, but when was the last time you had good chocolate on good bread? There is no one way to do it. Put a piece of good chocolate on a piece of good bread, and eat it. You can butter the bread first. Alternatively, toast the piece of bread, grate your favorite chocolate on top of it, and let it melt a little onto the warm bread. Top with strong olive oil and maybe a little salt.

Or, place pieces of chocolate on top of the bread and give it a minute under the broiler or in a toaster oven so the chocolate just starts to melt. Or make a chocolate sandwich.

BACCALÀ MANTECATO, OR WHIPPED SALT COD

Serves 4 or more as a starter or light entrée

INGREDIENTS

10.5 ounces (300 grams) thin pieces soaked baccalà (see headnote)

2–3 bay leaves

Small handful whole black peppercorns

1 small boiled peeled potato (russet or Yukon Gold, nothing waxy)

1–2 garlic cloves, minced

½–¾ cup (125–175 ml) olive oil

Toasted or grilled bread for serving

Salt, as needed

Freshly ground black pepper (optional)

Most closely associated with Venice, this salt cod dish is often served on planks of grilled or fried polenta, but bread is a common—and, in my opinion, superior—substitute. Related to the better-known "brandade" of French cooking, this version omits dairy for a cleaner, lighter taste and is easier on the garlic. You want to taste the baccalà and be able to enjoy the quality of the olive oil you are using.

Although you will probably start with about a pound of baccalà (typically how it is sold), a few days before you want to make this dish, use sharp kitchen scissors or a knife to cut off the thin flappy parts and remove any remaining skin. Save the thick loin portion for another recipe. Place the thinner portions in a container large enough to hold them and cover them with water. Refrigerate. You want to soak the salt cod for two or three days, changing the water at least once a day.

Instructions

Cut the soaked cod into four or five pieces. Place in a shallow, wide pan with the bay leaves (to taste) and black peppercorns and cover with cold water. Bring to a boil, then immediately reduce the heat to a simmer.

Poach the cod for a few minutes until it flakes easily. Don't overdo it; salt cod gets tougher when you cook it too much. Remove the pieces of fish from the cooking water (reserving the water, and leaving the peppercorns and bay leaves in the pan), and add to the bowl of a stand mixer fitted with the paddle attachment.

Toss in the boiled potato if using, and the minced garlic (to taste). Beat on low speed to break up the fish and combine. At this point, slowly drizzle in the olive oil →

in a steady stream with the mixer still running, as if you were making a mayonnaise. Slightly increase the speed of the mixer as you continue to add the oil. You may not need all of it. If the mixture is too thick, thin it with a little of the cooking water. You are looking for a light, fluffy, spreadable consistency that retains the texture of the fish. The oil should be completely emulsified with the fish, not too wet or too thick. (The potato helps with this.) Taste for salt and add a little if you need it. This makes a generous 2 cups.

CIAMBOTTA

Serves 2

Ciambotta is a homey, summer-inspired, southern Italian vegetable stew. The ways to make it are varied and flexible; you can pretty much alter it to suit your tastes or to use whatever ingredients you have on hand. That said, I urge you to show a little restraint, because your food will be better for it.

My favorite way to make this dish is slowly, perhaps over three or four hours, in a clay pot set over a simmer mat, without much fussing. In that case, I suggest starting early in the day and either reheating it before serving or enjoying it at room temperature when the flavors have really come together. You want to stir it just enough to keep it from sticking. Low enough heat, good olive oil, and the right cooking vessel should help with this. You can cook it in a metal pot (preferably enameled cast iron), and it will cook faster if you cut the vegetables a little smaller; do what works for you. But the more gently you cook my ciambotta, the better its flavor will be.

About those vegetables: I cut them into fairly large pieces to stand up to long cooking without getting mushy. They'll definitely soften, but it's nice when they retain some shape while still achieving a silken texture. I don't add liquid, so the vegetables cook in their own juices.

I also suggest lightly salting at various stages of cooking, which helps to build more depth of flavor and reduces the chances of the salt getting too concentrated as everything cooks down.

Some cooks add olives or capers to this dish toward the end of cooking, but I prefer to let the flavors of good summer produce speak for themselves. You can serve ciambotta topped with a soft-boiled or fried egg and even a little grated cheese for a more extravagant version. However you decide to go about it, the dish is not complete without good bread.

INGREDIENTS

2 medium red onions, cut top to bottom into ¼-inch slices

1 garlic clove, halved

Olive oil

Salt

4–5 small yellow-fleshed potatoes, such as Yukon Gold

1 medium or 2 small eggplant

3–4 thin-skinned long sweet peppers, or bell peppers if you must

2 ripe tomatoes or 3–4 canned whole peeled tomatoes

2 small zucchini

A spoonful of strattu (Sicilian-style tomato paste, see page xxxi) or a few spoonfuls of tomato puree

A few fresh basil leaves

Freshly ground black pepper

Thick slices of bread, for serving

Instructions

Combine the onions and garlic in a large pot (see above). Pour in a little oil, lightly salt, stir to coat, and cover, →

starting on low heat. (If you're using a clay pot, you have to introduce temperature changes gradually or you can crack your pot.) As the pot begins to warm and the onions and garlic start cooking, start to prep the potatoes, eggplant, sweet peppers, tomatoes, and zucchini. Every 3 or 4 minutes, give the onions and garlic a stir.

Rinse and peel the potatoes, then cut them into 1-inch wedges. Place in a bowl of cold water. Cut the eggplant into large chunks, placing them in a bowl of salted, acidulated water as you work. Stem and seed the sweet peppers, cutting them in strips as needed. Thin the strattu with a few spoonfuls of water in a small bowl. (If you are using tomato puree, skip this step.)

Boil a pot of water and fill a large bowl with water and ice cubes. Score the bottoms of each tomato with a shallow X and drop them into the water for a minute or two, then transfer them to an ice water bath. Drain, then discard the loosened skins. Cut the tomatoes in half, and discard the cores and seeds. (Skip this step for canned tomatoes.) Cut the zucchini into ¼-inch-thick rounds.

Go back to your onions and garlic. Once they have cooked down and are noticeably softer and sweet-smelling—about 20 minutes—stir in the thinned strattu (if using tomato puree, hold off). Cover and cook for another 5 minutes or so.

Drain the potatoes and the eggplant; add them to the pot, salt lightly, and stir to coat. Cover and cook, stirring only every so often.

Once the potatoes are partially cooked—20 to 30 minutes or more, depending on how low the heat on your stove actually is and how well the lid fits on your pot—add the peppers. (If you are using tomato puree, add it now.) Stir to coat, salt lightly, cover, and cook for another 20 minutes or so.

Add the tomatoes and zucchini. Lightly salt again. Give the stew a stir, cover, and walk away again, for 30 minutes or so. Once the zucchini has softened, and the potatoes are just cooked through, remove from the heat. Add a few torn basil leaves and season generously with the black pepper. Finish with a thin drizzle of olive oil—or wait until you have portioned it into shallow bowls on thick slices of grilled bread.

EGGS IN PURGATORY

Serves 2

Recipes for eggs poached in tomato sauce appear in some form or another in just about all tomato-eating cultures—and you can't eat eggs that way without bread. Toasting bread that is a few days old is a natural choice here, for soaking up the sauce and creating a worthy raft for the eggs.

Instructions

Thinly slice the garlic. Stem and seed the hot pepper, then finely chop. Pour in just enough oil to coat the bottom of a sauté pan, then add the garlic and start the heat at medium-low.

Once the garlic begins to sizzle, add the hot pepper, along with a little juice from the canned tomatoes. Crush the tomatoes by hand and add them to the pan. Season with salt.

Increase the heat to medium-high; cook for 6 to 8 minutes, stirring occasionally, to form a somewhat thickened, reduced sauce that's not too chunky. Use the back of a soup spoon to make two slight depressions on the surface. Crack 1 egg into a small bowl, then slip it into one of the depressions; repeat with the other egg. Season the eggs with salt and slightly reduce the heat to allow the eggs to poach in the sauce for 2 to 3 minutes, or to your desired doneness. You may want to cover the pan for this step.

While the eggs cook, heat another pan over medium-high heat. Film the hot pan with oil and fry/toast the bread on both sides. (Alternatively, you can lightly brush the bread with oil and grill it under the broiler.)

Place the toasted bread in a shallow serving bowl. Once the eggs are set, spoon the eggs and sauce on top of the bread, taking care to also transfer the eggs intact. Top with the shavings of Pecorino.

INGREDIENTS

1 garlic clove

1 small hot red chile pepper (dried, fresh, or packed in oil)

Olive oil

One 28-ounce can (about 3 cups/800 grams) peeled whole Italian tomatoes with their juices

Salt

2 eggs

1 slice of rustic bread, 1–1½ inches thick (from a largish loaf, a few days old)

Aged Pecorino, shaved

CLAMS ON FRISELLE
OR TOAST

Serves 2

Start with three or four dozen clams and a couple of rusks or Friselle (page 19) or some old bread. Wash the clams and clean out all the sand. Put them in a pot and steam them. Remove them as they open, about 10 minutes, discarding any that do not open.

Take half the clams out of their shells and chop them. Then, in a separate pan, put a little bit of garlic, a little dried chile pepper, and a pour of olive oil: When the garlic starts to sizzle, throw in a splash of white wine and let it cook off. (You can also save some of the clam juice from steaming and add that, but you'd want to strain it and, since it's very salty, know it's going to reduce and make your dish even saltier.) Then add some tomato—cherry tomatoes or a smaller tomato variety, but not too many. Cook that down for another 10 minutes or so. Then put in all the chopped clams and the whole clams in their shells. Turn off the heat, add some fresh parsley, then ladle all over friselle or sliced pieces of dried bread so it can absorb the liquid. Serve.

ROAST CHICKEN WITH BREAD OR TOAST

Serves 2 to 4

INGREDIENTS

One 4-pound chicken, giblets bundle removed

Salt

Coarsely ground black pepper

2 small lemons, preferably organic and unwaxed

Olive oil

4–6 slices of rustic bread, 1–1½ inches thick (from a largish loaf; see headnote)

Arguably, the greatest part of roasting a chicken for dinner is dredging bread through the accumulated juices and fat at the bottom of the roasting pan and eating it—way better than the chicken itself, I say.

This recipe takes that idea and makes it an all-in-one situation for sharing with guests, instead of eating your chicken drippings on bread, alone in the kitchen, before the rest of the meal goes to the table.

There are a lot of approaches to roast chicken with bread. For this one, I adapted Marcella Hazan's Roast Chicken with Lemons recipe, a favorite of mine. You can use fresh bread here, but two or three days stale might be even better. Serve with a green salad.

Instructions

Position a rack in the upper third of the oven; preheat to 350°F.

Thoroughly rinse the chicken inside and out. Dry it completely with clean kitchen towels or paper towels. Marcella advises the removal of any bits of fat. I do not; you want those to render onto the bread.

Aggressively season the bird inside and out with salt and pepper, rubbing the seasoning in with your hands.

Rinse the lemons, roll them on the counter while applying a little pressure to loosen their juices, then prick them all over with a fork. Insert them into the chicken cavity.

Use some oil to liberally grease the bottom of a roasting pan, then lay the slices of bread flat to cover the bottom. Pour about ¼ inch of water into the pan; this will prevent the bread from toasting too quickly. Set a roasting rack over the bread and place the chicken on the rack, →

breast side down. Roast on the upper oven rack for
30 minutes.

Remove the roasting pan from the oven. Remove the rack
holding the chicken so you can turn over all the pieces of
bread (for even toasting). Reposition the rack in the pan.
Use clean towels to grab the chicken and turn it over on
the rack, so the breast side is up. Return the pan to the
oven and roast for 30 more minutes.

Increase the heat to 400°F; roast for an additional
20 minutes, or until the skin is nicely golden and the juices
run clear when the thickest part of the thigh is pierced, or
until that same part of the thigh registers 165°F on a probe
thermometer.

Remove the roasting pan from the oven. Use more clean
towels to carefully lift and tilt the chicken off the rack so
its juices fall onto the toasted bread below, then transfer
the bird to a cutting board to rest for 10 minutes. Retrieve
and reserve the lemons.

To serve, arrange the bread slices on a platter. Carve the
chicken, placing its pieces atop the bread. Cut open
the lemons and carefully squeeze their hot juice over
the chicken and bread.

Variation

A fun summertime variation inspired by Frank Ruta, the
former White House chef of the late Palena, Annabelle,
and a handful of D.C. restaurants: Follow the recipe as
written above, but instead of using thick-sliced bread, tear
it into large, craggy pieces (croutons). Give them a stir
periodically as you tend to the chicken.

Once the chicken is done, toss the hot croutons with
1 pound or so of halved ripe cherry tomatoes, some thinly
sliced red onion, a spoonful or two of salted, well-rinsed
capers, and abundant chopped fresh flat-leaf parsley.
Squeeze the lemons from the inside of the bird onto the
bread and vegetables. Taste and adjust the seasoning, as
needed, and serve alongside the carved chicken.

SANDWICHES

A few notes about sandwiches

It would be terribly remiss of me to write a book about eating bread without including some mention of sandwiches. Initially, I didn't want them in here. The majority of recipes in this book focus on using and enjoying old bread. Sandwiches are almost always better eaten on fresh bread except in the case of being toasted or pressed. How great would it be to have an entire treatise devoted to old, dry bread? (I would enjoy it...along with the maybe 12 people who would buy such a book.)

But how to compose a recipe for a sandwich? Everyone can make a sandwich, right? It is probably the most popular way to eat bread, and, at the very least, I want to share some general guidelines as well as what might be a different perspective on the matter.

We live in a depressing era of Instagram-driven food trends, where so many sandwiches have become grotesque aberrations—oozing, dripping, hulking, overstuffed monsters, designed to be photographed as much as or more than they were designed to be eaten. I propose a modest revolution in the face of this excess: a return to the notion that sandwiches first and foremost are about the bread. I would like to dispel the idea that the bread in a sandwich is merely a vehicle that prevents you from getting condiments on your fingers or eating meat with your hands. Plain and simple: bad bread means bad sandwiches.

We have arrived at this strange place as a culture due to generations of having to accept terrible bread because not much else was readily available. Generally speaking, bread in many places in the United States hasn't been good enough to enjoy on its own, or even modestly dressed as a sandwich. Spongy, industrial bread tastes bad or at best bland, and the more stuff you can pack inside of it, the less you are aware that you are actually eating it. From a functionality standpoint, however, this type of soft bread does allow a certain flexibility in the construction of a sandwich.

It also does not present any opposition to smushing it down and cramming it in your mouth. This, and a morbid fixation with the tastes of suburban childhoods, have created the wild popularity/ubiquity of Martin's Potato Rolls and other industrial bread products that depend on dough conditioners and preservatives for their celebrated squishiness and incredibly long shelf life. I get it: I've smushed and crammed in this kind of bread product as much as the next guy. But really, let's not forget we have teeth.

Truly, texture is an extremely important consideration in choosing the bread for a sandwich. Ask yourself: Will I be able to bite through this sandwich? Will chewing this sandwich be a pleasure or incredibly laborious? Hard-crusted "country style" loaves are not always the ideal choice when it comes to sandwiches. When you slice them horizontally and fill them hoagie-style, sometimes they can be too much of a workout. Even sliced normally, the crust can be too thick and the interior too soft to provide the right construction. That bread is often better for sandwiches when toasted or pressed, or perhaps cut thick and served open-faced, topped with a filling particularly wet and best eaten with a knife and fork. (Yes, it is fair to debate whether this is still considered a sandwich; for the sake of discussion, I say sure, why not?)

Personally, my favorite bread for sandwiches is pizza bianca (page 25). When made well, it is perfectly crisp (not crunchy—there is a difference) and sturdy enough to be laden with a wide range of fillings while remaining simultaneously soft, light, flavorful, and incredibly digestible. Focaccia can also be a great choice, as well as ciabatta, or even a good baguette. The key in choosing either of the latter two is finding versions that are light and airy—not excessively bready—with crusts that are neither too hard nor too thick.

About the wide range of options for bread and filling: Think about what they are like to eat before you select any. It sounds silly, but it is astounding how many sandwiches made on the wrong bread are sold in celebrated commercial contexts. Another related consideration is structure. Will this bread adequately stand up to the intended fillings? Make sure you are not asking too much of the bread with a filling that is just excessive or ill-conceived. A meatball sandwich can be great, but probably not on brioche or a soft pan de mie. The bread will start to dissolve with the sauce and there's a good chance the meatballs will fall out.

Seek harmony and balance in both construction and flavor. Regarding sandwich fillings, that's key. Pick one to three items (in extreme cases four) and balance them in proportion to each other. Choose ones that will serve and highlight the good bread you have.

Season the components of a sandwich separately. It is always disappointing when you bite into a sandwich with lettuce and/or tomato or other vegetables and those items are not salted or seasoned at all. A little salt makes a difference. Olive oil is always a good idea—a light drizzle on the bread or to dress any vegetable goes a long way toward making a sandwich that is merely fine into one that is way better.

HAM SANDWICH

Serves 1

No one needs to be told how to make a ham sandwich. Slice a loaf of bread somewhat thinly and fill it with the preferred ham of your choosing. Easy on the condiments and add-ons. Let the ham and the bread do the talking.

We sometimes offer a ham sandwich at Bread and Salt because I love the Praga ham from Salumeria Biellese— a wholesaler based in Hackensack, New Jersey, with a location in Manhattan—so much I wanted to give it a home.

If you don't know about Praga ham, you should. Technically, under European law, any Prague ham produced outside of the Czech Republic should be referred to as "Prague-style ham." Praga is the Italian form, but regardless of what you call it and where it comes from, it is a brine-cured, cooked, and lightly smoked ham and it is fantastic for sandwiches and for eating in general.

We slice it relatively thin on the slicer, but not too thin; because since it is cooked, it is softer than a prosciutto crudo or a Spanish ham, and it is pleasurable if the slices have a bit of body. We then drape them loosely and amply on a piece of freshly baked bread made with stone-milled flour, dress them with olive oil, top them with another slice of bread, and that is it. It's worth seeking out and will exceed your expectations of any ham sandwich.

PANE CUNZATO

Serves 1 to 4

Pane cunzato—"dressed bread"—is famously associated with western Sicily and is often served at the bakeries around the island.

At its most simple, a freshly baked loaf of semolina bread is split horizontally while still hot, doused in olive oil, and seasoned with dried oregano and a little salt. More common and more delicious, ripe tomatoes are added with a few fillets of anchovies and a little primosale, a very young sheep's-milk cheese. Maybe a few capers. Variations are endless, but the anchovy, tomato, and oregano with fresh cheese is classic and certainly my favorite. The sandwiches are made ahead of time so all the oil and tomato and anchovy flavor has time to really soak into the bread. That's part of the magic.

If large tomatoes aren't fantastic where you live, cherry tomatoes will often be better. Select the sweetest, juiciest tomatoes you can find and crush or tear them over the bread instead of cutting them. You want the juices in the bread, not on your cutting board. When it's not tomato season, or you don't have access to great tomatoes, either save this sandwich for another day or use excellent-quality dried or partially dried tomatoes preserved in oil. Go easy though, because they can be strong-tasting and the good ones are pretty expensive.

Primosale is traditional, but it can be hard to find, or when you do find it, it often has started to get a little funky, losing the characteristics that make it so great as a fresh cheese. If you can't find a good one, use Crotonese, Toscano, or Sardo Pecorino instead.

Instructions

Unless you have a really great relationship with your local baker, or you are willing to get up super early (this sandwich would be worth it), you might have difficulty getting a loaf of bread steaming hot from the oven. If

INGREDIENTS

1 loaf freshly baked bread, preferably semolina

Olive oil—the best quality you have

Salt

Freshly ground black pepper

Dried oregano, preferably Sicilian, on the branch

3–4 large peak-season, ripe tomatoes, sliced

8 ounces (150 grams) primosale cheese (see headnote), thinly sliced

10–15 salted anchovy fillets, well rinsed

you can't get bread that fresh, get it as fresh as you can and heat it whole in your oven at home until its interior is pretty hot. You can wrap it in foil first if you want to protect the crust.

Split the loaf horizontally (lengthwise). If the crumb of the bread isn't super open, make a series of quick, shallow cuts to the crumb on both sides of the bread or snip it in a few places with scissors to allow the seasoning to further penetrate. You're opening up surface area to allow the bread to absorb more oil and become more flavorful.

While the bread is steaming hot, liberally pour oil on both cut sides. Season with a little salt, pepper, and crumbled oregano. Layer the tomato slices across the bottom piece of the bread, then top with cheese slices. Distribute the anchovy fillets (to taste) across the cheese and close the sandwich with the top half of the seasoned bread, pressing it gently. Let it sit for a little bit to let all of the flavors soak in before eating. Cut into individual portions and serve.

PANE E MORTADELLA

Serves 2

This is arguably the greatest bologna sandwich of all time. It's not any more complicated than its name. It's an ideal, perfect marriage. Simplicity! Elegance!

Split open a couple of pizza bianca, focaccia, ciabatta, rosette, or pane soffiato if you can find them (hand-size)... hell, even a kaiser roll if you live near a bakery that makes an excellent one. Or use any really good bread that's fit for a sandwich.

Get a few very thin slices of mortadella (see Resources, page 225). It's worth seeking out the good stuff. Don't go overboard; use just enough to balance the bread.

Keep your aioli, pickled whatever, vegetables, and even cheese away from this sandwich. If your bread is good and your mortadella is good, you would be doing them a tragic disservice. Trust me.

INGREDIENTS

Pizza bianca, focaccia, ciabatta, rosette, or pane soffiato (see headnote)

Olive oil—the best that you have

A few very thin slices of good mortadella

Instructions

Split open the bread. Drizzle a bit of olive oil, judiciously, on the split sides, if you are so inclined. You'll lay in the slices of mortadella with a few folds to give them some volume. You don't want a flat stack.

GRILLED MARINATED ZUCCHINI SANDWICH WITH STRACCIATELLA AND MINT

Serves 2

This recipe is great for summer zucchini season when you feel like firing up the grill. (I suggest trying to find costata romanesco zucchini, but really any zucchini will work if they are not monstrous.) The grilled zucchini needs to marinate for a few hours, or overnight in the refrigerator.

Instructions

Cut the zucchini lengthwise into slices slightly less than ¼ inch thick. If you really want to go the extra mile, lay out the slices on a rack at room temperature for an hour or two to help them dry out a little. This makes for better grilling, but it isn't strictly necessary.

Use a pastry brush to coat them lightly with olive oil. Alternatively, you can toss them in a bowl with a small amount of oil and salt. You don't want them dripping with oil; be moderate here.

Take the zucchini to your extremely hot grill. Lay the slices flat on the grate and grill for about a minute or so on each side. You want some char on these, but you don't want them to entirely mush out. Transfer them to a bowl with the garlic, lemon juice, and a handful of mint leaves. Season with salt and pepper. Add a glug of olive oil. Adjust the ratios to your taste, but I suggest that you want this heavy on the lemon and the mint.

Allow the grilled zucchini to marinate at room temperature for a few hours if you plan on making your sandwiches later that same day, or cover and place overnight in the refrigerator. If the grilled zucchini is chilled, let it come to room temperature for at least an hour before proceeding.

INGREDIENTS

4 zucchini, no more than 6 inches long

Olive oil

1 garlic clove, thinly sliced

Juice of 2–3 lemons

Abundant fresh spearmint leaves (commonly labeled as "mint" in grocery stores)

Salt

Freshly ground black pepper

Stracciatella

Fresh focaccia, pizza bianca, or other good soft-but-sturdy sandwich bread

When you are ready to assemble your sandwiches, split open your bread. Remove the zucchini slices from the marinade, leaving the now sad-looking mint and the garlic behind. Lay the zucchini across the bottom bread halves. Top with a few fresh mint leaves, a drizzle of the marinade, and the stracciatella. Drizzle a little marinade on the cut side of the top bread halves before closing, then cut each sandwich in half.

This is supposed to be messy. Use lots of napkins.

ANCHOVY, CHICORY, AND PROVOLA

Serves 1

This is another anchovy sandwich that will help you grow to love them. Provola and scamorza are lightly aged pasta-filata cheeses—soft, fresh cheese that's often made from curd—that are firmer and drier than mozzarella and not nearly as sharp as provolone. (See Resources, page 225.)

Instructions

Preheat an oven or toaster oven to about 450°F. Split open your sandwich bread.

Place a few thin slices of provola or scamorza on the bottom piece of the bread. Place both pieces of bread, cut side and cheese side up, separately in the oven or toaster oven (don't sandwich them together).

Toast until the cheese is just beginning to melt and lose its edges. Don't brown it. Meanwhile, dress the chicory leaves with a little salt, pepper, lemon juice, and olive oil. You want them to be bright-tasting, but not dripping wet.

Lay the anchovy fillets (to taste) on top of the melted cheese. Top with the dressed chicory and eat.

INGREDIENTS

Sandwich-size piece of pizza bianca, focaccia, or particularly good ciabatta

A few thin slices of provola or scamorza

Small inner leaves of a head of Castelfranco chicory (or substitute tender escarole, frisée, Belgian endive, or radicchio)

Salt

Freshly ground black pepper

Fresh lemon juice

Olive oil

4 (or as many or few as you'd like) anchovy fillets, preferably from 2–3 whole salted anchovies, rinsed, cleaned, and filleted (see page xxxi)

FRIED EGGPLANT SANDWICH

Serves 2

I could have included at least ten ways to enjoy eggplant on a sandwich. It may just be the king of vegetables. For the sake of brevity, I chose just this one.

Another variety of eggplant besides the globe can work here as well—just select a ripe one in the peak of the season that is firm and supple with thin, taut skin that preferably hasn't spent too much time in a refrigerator.

Instructions

Cut off the eggplant's stem, then cut the eggplant crosswise into slices about ¼ inch thick. Salt each side of each slice and place in a colander. Allow to sit for 30 minutes to 1 hour; the salt will draw moisture out of the eggplant slices.

While your eggplant is undergoing its salt treatment, quarter or halve the cherry tomatoes (depending on size), and thinly slice the red onion. Place the tomatoes and onions in a bowl with the mint leaves. Lightly salt and dress with a few drops of olive oil and a squeeze of juice from the lemon, and allow this to sit so the flavors can marry and the tomatoes will give up some juice.

Return to your eggplant when enough time has passed. Rinse off the salt extremely well, then rinse it again and maybe a third time (if you don't wash the slices extremely well, the eggplant might be too salty). Dry the slices well and press them with a clean, dry kitchen towel to make sure there is no moisture left.

Fill a skillet with ½ to 1 inch of oil and heat the oil to about 340°F. (You can test it to see if it's hot enough by tossing in a crouton-size piece of bread to see if it fries.) Gently slip a few (very dry) eggplant slices into the oil. Don't crowd them. Fry until a pleasant shade of light brown, 3 to 4 minutes, flipping them once midway

INGREDIENTS

1 medium globe eggplant
(about a pound)

Salt

1 half-pint cherry tomatoes
(the sweetest variety you can find)

Half of a small red onion

6 or so fresh mint leaves

Olive oil

Half a lemon

Focaccia, pizza bianca, ciabatta, or other good sandwich bread (for focaccia and bianca, use about a hand-size serving per sandwich)

through. Drain the fried slices on a rack set over some paper towels. Lightly press with more paper towels to extract any excess oil. Eat one and see whether it is salty enough. If it needs it, give the rest some salt.

Cut open your sandwich bread and lay a few warm slices of fried eggplant across the bottom half. Spoon the tomato salad mixture—juice included—on top of the eggplant. Complete with the top half of the bread, cut the sandwich in half, and eat.

You might end up with a lot of extra eggplant slices, so make another sandwich—or just eat them as they are, if you haven't already.

ROASTED QUINCE, PECORINO, AND ARUGULA

Serves 2

INGREDIENTS

1 lemon

3 firm quince

1 bay leaf

A few whole black peppercorns

2 whole cloves

Salt

Splash of good-quality white wine

Honey

Your choice of sandwich bread slices (I use pizza bianca, but you can use focaccia or the sandwich bread of your choice)

A chunk of aged Pecorino

A few small (but not baby) leaves of arugula

Olive oil

Coarsely ground black pepper

It doesn't make a ton of sense to go through all the labor involved in preparing quince, available in late fall, to make just one sandwich. So either invite a friend or two over and make sandwiches for everyone, or save the extra to serve as a side dish with some pork or game—or even as a dessert if you want to doctor it up a little and pair it with whipped ricotta or ice cream.

For the cheese here, use the most significant Pecorino you can find—something complex and a little nutty, that makes for a good table cheese. You want something with some age on it, but one that's not too sharp or dry.

Instructions

Preheat the oven to 250°F. Use a vegetable peeler to remove the lemon peel in wide swaths, with no pith. Cut the lemon in half and squeeze its juice into a large bowl of water.

Rinse the quince, then peel, cut in half, and use a paring knife or sturdy spoon to remove the core and seeds. Place the cut quince in your lemon water as you work, to keep it from oxidizing.

Place all the quince halves in a shallow baking dish, cut sides down, with the bay leaf, peppercorns, cloves, swaths of lemon peel, a pinch of salt, white wine, and enough water to come just partway up the sides of the quince (don't submerge them).

Very lightly drizzle with honey. You don't want to make the fruit sweet; use just enough to take off the quince's tart edge and amplify its natural perfume. Cover tightly with foil and place in the oven. Slow-roast for about 2 to 3 hours, turning them over toward the end of cooking. →

Check them somewhat more frequently as time passes. You don't want them to mush out, but you do want them to be softly colored, somewhere from pink to red, and tender enough to pierce with a fork. You don't want to eat undercooked quince—trust me. Make sure the pan liquid isn't evaporating too much (you want the juices, so add a little more water as needed). When the quince is almost finished, remove the foil and give the fruit a little more time in the oven.

Remove from the oven and allow them to cool in the now somewhat syrupy liquid; taste and adjust seasoning as needed. Cut the quince halves into slices about ⅛ inch thick and layer them across the bottom pieces of your bread. Drizzle with a little of the syrupy liquid.

Thinly shave (not grate) a little of the Pecorino on top of the quince. Use enough to know it's there, but remember you aren't making cheese sandwiches. Top each with the arugula, a thread of olive oil, salt, and a little pepper before completing the sandwiches.

BROCCOLI RABE

Serves 1

Sandwiches are often better when they don't have meat.
This is not a radical idea. For the cheese here, try an
aged Pecorino Moliterno, Pecorino Canestrato, or even a
Pecorino Romano from Lazio (not Sardinia).

Instructions

Bring a large pot of water to a boil. Salt it generously.
Fill a large bowl with water and ice cubes.

Add the broccoli rabe and cook for a minute or so,
just until it is a slightly brighter green. Use tongs to
immediately transfer it to the ice water bath. Once it has
cooled, drain and coarsely chop. Discard the cooking
water.

Crush the garlic, then place it in a skillet with a film of
olive oil, over low heat. Press the garlic into the pan with
a wooden spoon. As soon as the garlic begins to sizzle,
add the hot pepper and the still-damp chopped broccoli
rabe. Season with salt and increase the heat to medium.
Drag the rabe around in the pan until it is cooked to your
liking—though for sandwich purposes, cooking it a little
on the soft side (but not obliterated) is good. Taste for
seasoning, then discard the garlic clove and the hot pepper
(if left whole).

Split your sandwich bread. Scoop out some of its interior
crumb as needed (and reserve for another use, as bread
crumbs, pancotto, you name it). Add a smear of the ricotta
on one side of the bread, top generously with the warm
broccoli rabe, grate a little Pecorino over it, and drizzle
with more olive oil before eating.

INGREDIENTS

Salt

1 small bunch broccoli rabe,
tough stem ends trimmed

1 garlic clove

Olive oil

1 small fresh or dried hot chile
pepper (whole or chopped; the
latter will make the dish spicier)

Ciabatta, baguette, focaccia, or a
serviceable roll (semolina is nice)

Ricotta (see Resources, page 225)

Small piece of aged Pecorino

PEPPER AND POTATO

Serves 2 to 4

I understand that to most contemporary Americans living outside of Pittsburgh, the idea of putting potatoes on a sandwich is just plain crazy. I assure you it isn't. It's actually enjoyed in many parts of the world in many different combinations. Try it. You might like it. Who doesn't like carbs?

This is a common side dish in Calabria, Italy, that also happens to make a great sandwich filling. If you like, make just the filling and serve with your dinner, save the leftovers, and the following day stuff them into bread for lunch.

For the peppers, use a mix of colors and types, if you'd like—and make sure they're good ones. I like elongated sweet peppers like Carmens. For the potatoes, Yukon Golds will work. German butterballs and Picassos are also interesting varieties. Experiment with what's available to you—just look for something creamy and relatively low moisture. For the bread, get something with a decent yet light crust.

INGREDIENTS

1 small red onion

Olive oil

2 or 3 sweet peppers (see headnote)

Salt

4 medium yellow-fleshed potatoes (see headnote)

Bread with a light crust, such as a roll or focaccia

Instructions

Cut the onion from top to bottom into slices between ⅛ and ¼ inch thick (it doesn't really matter, just not too thin). Place them in a wide skillet with an abundant amount of good olive oil (a little more than you might be comfortable with, but not too much; think shallow-fry, heavier than a light film). Bring the heat up to medium or so.

Stem the peppers and discard the seeds and any ribs inside. Cut into strips about ½ inch thick. Once the onion slices have begun to soften, add the peppers and season with a little salt. Cook, stirring regularly and monitoring the heat. You don't want the onions and peppers to get too brown. →

Meanwhile, rinse, peel, and cut the potatoes into small wedges or rounds, roughly the same size as the peppers so they don't take too long to cook. Once the peppers have begun to soften, add the potatoes and some more salt. Cook, stirring periodically to prevent excess sticking and to promote some browning of the potatoes. Adjust the heat as needed; you want all the vegetables to be soft, about 25 minutes. Taste, and adjust the salt. Spoon onto your sliced bread and eat warm or at room temperature.

MOZZARELLA EN CARROZZA

Serves 2

This is the greatest of all grilled cheese sandwiches.

In Italy, it is typically made with pancarre or pane in cassetta, which is basically white sandwich bread. It should not be the flavorless, packaged kind found in an American grocery store aisle; choose a naturally leavened Pullman loaf from your local bakery instead. You also can opt for a more rustic-style loaf depending on the breadth of its cross-section and whether the crumb is relatively soft and not irregularly holed. (This is not the best use for dense, Germanic rye breads or really airy ciabatta.) A rustic loaf might be harder to cut evenly, however, and you will need to carve a good square or rectangle out of each slice. Whichever bread you use, make sure it is relatively fresh—no more than a day or two old, with some moisture and life in the crumb.

The sandwich pairs nicely with a simple green salad or with figs and a drizzle of honey.

INGREDIENTS

Olive oil, or your preferred oil for pan-frying

All-purpose flour

1 egg, beaten

Finely ground Toasted Bread Crumbs (page 125)

Fior di latte, thinly sliced—as much as you want per sandwich

2 salted anchovy fillets, rinsed well (optional, but if you ditch the anchovies, be prepared to add salt)

4 slices of bread, each about ¼ inch thick, crusts removed (see headnote)

Instructions

Heat about ½ inch of oil to about 340°F in a pan large enough to hold two sandwiches.

Meanwhile, place the flour, beaten egg, and bread crumbs in three separate, shallow dishes.

Divide the cheese evenly between two slices of bread without letting any of it hang over the edges. Place an anchovy fillet, if using, on each portion of cheese, then top with the remaining bread slices to form two sandwiches, pressing down to seal them.

Dredge each sandwich—on all sides, edges included—lightly with flour, then egg, then coat completely with the bread crumbs. Test the oil by throwing in a corner of bread to see if it fries. If it's ready, fry the sandwiches in the hot oil, turning on all sides, just until golden brown and crisp.

Let the sandwiches drain and cool on a wire rack set over paper towels before serving, though you'll want to serve them warm.

TUNA WITH HARISSA, EGGS, AND OLIVES

Serves 1

All the other sandwiches listed in this book are at least vaguely Italianate, if not actually classically Italian in origin. This sandwich is an exception.

In Tunisia, this is pretty much the number one sandwich, and it is pretty great. Known as "fricassée" in French, the sandwich is typically served on something akin to a savory doughnut. It is basically a piece of fried bread dough that is broken open and stuffed with oil-packed tuna, a smear of harissa, a quartered hard-cooked egg, and olives. Sometimes potatoes as well; variations abound. This combination is so prevalent in Tunisia that almost all sandwiches, and many other dishes, are also topped with tuna and harissa and olives as a garnish.

I suggest using a baguette, as it will be harder to find savory fried bread unless you want to make it yourself. Spring for the absolute best-quality oil-packed tuna you find; you'll be glad you did.

INGREDIENTS

1 egg

Salt

About 6 oil-cured black olives, or a mix of black and green

Half of a fresh, crisp baguette

Harissa (page 208)

1 can excellent-quality oil-packed tuna

Finely chopped fresh flat-leaf parsley (optional)

Minced red onion (optional)

Olive oil (optional)

Instructions

Boil the egg in generously salted boiling water for exactly 8½ minutes. Fill a large bowl with water and ice cubes. Plunge egg into an ice water bath. This gets you past a soft-boiled egg, but not quite all of the way to hard. It should still be a touch glossy in the middle, which will be more pleasant to eat. Peel and quarter lengthwise. Lightly salt.

Pit your olives.

Split the baguette in half lengthways down the side, but don't cut it all the way through. Use a spoon to smear harissa on one interior side of the bread. Be generous; it should be spicy to a degree that suits your taste.

Open the can of tuna and spoon all of it evenly inside of the bread, reserving some of its oil. Scatter the olives on top of the tuna, and place the egg quarters evenly along the length of the sandwich. Sprinkle with the parsley and minced red onion, if using, and drizzle the inside of the sandwich with a little oil from the tuna or some fresh olive oil. Close the sandwich and eat it.

FRITTATA WITH ARTICHOKE, PECORINO, AND MINT

INGREDIENTS

2 eggs

Salt

Freshly ground black pepper

Olive oil

Small crusty roll

A small piece of aged
Pecorino, thinly sliced

2–3 artichokes sott'olio, halved

Fresh mint leaves,
or mentuccia if available

Serves 1 or 2

For the cheese here, look for a Pecorino that's not too young and soft but not too hard—aged three to six months. A Pecorino Etrusco or a Crotonese would be nice.

Instructions

Use a fork to beat the eggs in a small bowl with a pinch of salt and pepper, and a small splash of water.

Heat a small skillet with a generous pour of olive oil over medium heat. Pour in the eggs; the oil should be hot enough that they start cooking right away. Use a wooden or flexible spatula to give them a stir, pushing and slightly lifting the curds to the center of the pan and letting the runny egg fall underneath. Reduce the heat slightly and cook until the bottom and the edges of the eggs are mostly set but the center is still soft. Use the spatula to make sure the edges aren't stuck and the bottom is not sticking and the eggs are somewhat nicely browned, but not dark.

Place a pan-size plate over the pan, then invert so the frittata lands cooked side up on the plate. Slide the frittata back into the pan (still cooked side up) and return to the heat to finish cooking, just a few minutes more. The frittata should be lightly browned and puffy and still a little soft inside, but cook it to your liking.

Drain it briefly on paper towels, then tuck it inside your split roll. Top with some thin slices of the cheese, the artichokes, a few mint leaves, a drizzle of olive oil, and an additional pinch of pepper, if you like.

I use pieces of old bread about as often as I use slices. Which is to say, a lot. Some of my favorite dishes are made with pieces of bread, like the recipes for pancotto, which translates to "cooked bread." And the meatballs made with pieces rather than crumbs are quietly revolutionary—so much so that they deserve their own section.

CROUTONS

Makes several cups

Croutons are large toasted bread crumbs, more or less. Like making my basic Toasted Bread Crumbs (page 125), making croutons mostly involves segmenting larger pieces of bread into smaller pieces of bread.

There are a few ways to go about this, depending on the condition and age of your bread and the ultimate destination of the crouton. If you store them in an airtight container in a dry place, croutons last forever.

You can also flavor your croutons with herbs, but I don't.

INGREDIENTS

Half a loaf of bread, older than a day, preferably several days old

Olive oil

Salt

Instructions

Preheat the oven to 400°F.

If the bread still has some softness and give to the crumb, pull it into different-size pieces with your hands, leaving most of the crust behind. Irregularity is important. Don't cube your old bread and make perfectly square or rectangular croutons, which look weird and feel strange when you eat them. In terms of size, make sure they are small enough to fit in your mouth easily.

Toss in a bowl with a healthy amount of olive oil and a little bit of salt. Not too much. The bread is probably already salted, and wherever the croutons will end up will most likely be salted as well. Bake on a sheet pan in the oven until golden brown and crisp. Periodically give the tray a shake or stir the croutons to ensure even cooking. This will take 10 minutes, or more likely 15, depending on how dry the bread is. Also, note that smaller pieces will be finished before larger ones. Variations in size will create a range of textures. Use as desired or enjoy as a snack.

Alternatively, if you have a completely hard, dried-out end of bread, wrap it in a towel and whack it with a rolling pin or some other heavy blunt object and smash it into small, irregular pieces roughly the size you want. Croutons made from older, drier bread have a harder and less yielding texture, delivering more crunch than crisp. As a result, they should be made slightly smaller than croutons made from fresher bread so they are a little easier on your jaws. Toss with olive oil and bake on a sheet pan at 400°F to the desired doneness. Though a little drier and harder, these store well and can hang out in a salad for more time without going limp and soggy.

STUFFED PEPPERS

Serves 2 to 4

Here's what I look for in peppers: First, I generally wait
until pepper season, which is late summer and into the
fall, before I make dishes that require peppers. Depending
on the dish and the style of peppers, I look for thick-
walled peppers, sweet peppers, and more tapered conical
peppers, rather than a sweet, round pepper, like a bell
pepper. For this dish, I like Carmen peppers, which
are becoming more prevalent at farmers markets, and
Escamillo peppers, which are related to Carmens. For
other dishes, I look for Cornito peppers, which are a bit
smaller; Marseilles peppers have incredible notes of citrus.
Jimmy Nardello is an incredible frying pepper, as are
shishitos, but I wouldn't stuff them.

Instructions

Preheat the oven to 400°F.

Soak the stale bread in just enough warm water or milk
to cover in a bowl until it softens. Rinse the salted capers,
then soak in a small bowl of water for 10 to 15 minutes
and drain. Rinse the whole salted anchovies, discard their
spines and fins, then coarsely chop the fillets.

Whisk the eggs in a large mixing bowl. Mince the garlic
and chop the parsley; add both to the eggs. Grate the
cheese into the mixture.

Once the bread has softened, squeeze out all excess
moisture and add to the bowl with the eggs and cheese.
Add the anchovies and the drained capers. Season with
salt and pepper.

Cut off the tops of the peppers (stem ends) and discard the
seeds, core, and any white ribs inside, being careful not to
break the pepper.

INGREDIENTS

1 cup (150 grams) stale bread
pieces (crusts removed)

Warm water or milk

1 tablespoon (5 grams) salted capers

2 whole salted anchovies
(see page xxxi)

2 eggs

1 garlic clove

8–10 sprigs fresh flat-leaf parsley

4 tablespoons (60 grams)
grated aged Pecorino

Salt

Freshly ground black pepper

6 horn-shaped red or yellow sweet
peppers, about 5 inches long

Olive oil for drizzling

Lightly salt the inside of the peppers. Use your fingers to fill each pepper with the bread mixture until it is mostly full. You want the stuffing to be a little loose because it will expand as it bakes.

Place the peppers in a shallow baking dish, drizzle with oil, season with salt, and roast for about 45 minutes to 1 hour—turning them at least once partway through—until the peppers are fully cooked, wrinkled, soft, and just starting to brown.

Serve warm.

CHERRY TOMATO SALAD WITH CROUTONS

Serves 2

Of course I am going to tell you to use the best possible cherry tomatoes at the peak of ripeness for this salad. It's really not worth making if you are just going to buy some flavorless specimens from the grocery store.

Instructions

Place the croutons in a bowl large enough to contain the rest of the salad ingredients. Cut the cherry tomatoes in half or, better yet, tear them in half over the bowl, letting the juices fall on the toasted croutons, and add them to the bowl.

If your onion slices are unpleasantly strong-tasting, soak them in a bowl of cold water with a drop of vinegar for about 10 minutes. Squeeze any excess water from the slices (or pat them with paper towels), then add to the tomatoes and croutons. Add your chile pepper in increments, tasting as you go. Toss in a few whole (or torn if large) mint or basil leaves, and season with salt. Taste; if your tomatoes lack the right amount of acidity, add the vinegar.

Dress the salad with olive oil, and toss. Allow it to sit for a moment so the croutons can soak up the juices from the tomatoes and the oil.

INGREDIENTS

A handful of Croutons (see page 88)

1 pint perfect red cherry tomatoes (25–30 total)

A few slices of red onion

1 small dried hot red chile pepper, seeded, stemmed, and finely chopped

A few fresh mint or basil leaves

Salt

A drop or two of red wine vinegar (optional)

Olive oil

Let's talk about farmers market tomatoes.

If you are the type of person who has been going to farmers markets for the past decade or so, you may have noticed that the variety of tomatoes available has shifted radically. Tomatoes are a huge moneymaker for small farms because people don't have to cook them. Anyone can go to the market, buy a great ripe tomato, cut it up, put some salt on it, and impress their friends.

The tomato is the king of the market season. As a result, more and more farmers try to extend the season on either end with hothouses so they can be the first to market with tomatoes and still have them after their competitors run out. It doesn't matter that these tomatoes aren't nearly as good. People are starved for that taste of summer, so they will buy them. And to differentiate themselves from competitors, farmers have taken to growing a much wider variety of tomatoes than ever before.

Fresh, local tomatoes at their peak aren't enough, apparently. Consumers demand heirloom tomatoes, or they at least want to think what they are getting are heirloom tomatoes. The actual variety and lineage of a particular plant, not to mention flavor, is less important than color for most consumers. "Is this tomato yellow? Orange? Striped? Polka-dotted?"

For farmers market vendors, the idea is that multicolored tomatoes make the market table more attractive and give the impression that they are heirloom tomatoes. The majority of tomatoes in these fiesta packs are hybrid tomatoes selected specifically for color, not for taste, not for quality. And on top of all that, in cases when people *are* thinking about flavor, even in the case of actual heirloom tomatoes, most gravitate toward low-acid, sweeter varieties.

What happened to tomatoes with the right balance of acidity and sweetness? Beautiful red cherry tomatoes? There are plenty of heirloom tomatoes that meet this description. Grow every damn type of tomato you want. But let me buy them separately and enjoy them for their individual qualities. I'll choose to mix them myself when I'm feeling festive.

PANCOTTO AL POMODORO

INGREDIENTS

Salt

5 pounds fresh ripe tomatoes

Olive oil

1 garlic clove, thinly sliced

1 small hot red chile pepper (fresh or dried), stemmed, seeded, and thinly sliced crosswise

1¼–1½ cups (200–250 grams) stale bread, crusts and all, torn into bite-size pieces

A few fresh basil leaves

Serves 2 or 3

Most Americans might be more familiar—in name at least—with the Tuscan variant of this dish known as pappa al pomodoro. Pancotto al pomodoro is pretty much the same, although the locals in Tuscany use their infamous unsalted bread. Versions are found all over Italy, as bread and tomatoes are one of life's most perfect pairings. In winter, this can be made with top-quality canned tomatoes, but I like it best with fresh tomatoes.

Instructions

Bring a large pot of water to a boil. Salt it generously. Fill a large bowl with water and ice cubes.

Use a sharp knife to score a shallow X at the bottom of each tomato. Working in batches, drop them into the boiling water. After a minute or two, use a slotted spoon to transfer them to the ice water bath to cool them quickly. Reserve the cooking water. Drain the tomatoes, then discard their loosened skins, seedy gel, and cores. Cut or tear into large chunks, over a bowl to catch the juices.

Coat a deep skillet with some oil, add the garlic and the hot pepper, and start the heat on low. Once the garlic begins to sizzle, toss in the pieces of bread, stirring to coat.

Add the chunks of tomatoes plus any accumulated juices. Season with salt and stir. Increase to a simmer, cooking for 10 to 20 minutes, until the bread has completely softened and become custardy, stirring and breaking up the pieces as you go. Taste for salt and add, as needed. Tear the basil leaves, letting them fall into the pan, and remove from the heat.

Serve in shallow bowls with a drizzle of oil.

PANCOTTO WITH BROCCOLI RABE

Serves 2 to 3

This variation on a humble soup features slightly bitter greens instead of beans. I like to make it slightly wetter and thicker than my Pancotto with Beans (see page 192).

Instructions

Bring a large pot of water to a boil. Salt it generously. Fill a large bowl with water and ice cubes.

Drop the broccoli rabe into the pot. Blanch it for a few minutes until bright green but still somewhat crisp. Use a slotted spoon to transfer to the ice water bath. Reserve the cooking water. Drain and coarsely chop the broccoli rabe.

Coat a medium to large sauté pan with oil, add the garlic, and start the heat on medium-low. Once the garlic begins to sizzle, add the hot pepper and the pieces of bread, stirring to coat. Do not let the garlic brown; add a splash of the reserved cooking water, as needed. Taste the cooking water; if it is too salty, dilute it with tap water before using it further.

Stir in the chopped broccoli rabe, then add enough of the reserved cooking water (around 4 cups) to completely cover the bread and rabe in the pan.

Reduce the heat to low and cook, uncovered, until the bread is soft, stirring occasionally to break up the pieces of bread as you go. Once the bread has completely softened and broken down, about 8 to 10 minutes, taste for seasoning. Add a little more of the cooking water if the consistency is too thick.

Serve in a shallow bowl or bowls with a drizzle of oil and the other dried hot pepper.

INGREDIENTS

Salt

1 bunch broccoli rabe, tough stem ends trimmed

Olive oil

1 garlic clove, thinly sliced

1 small hot red chile pepper (fresh, dried, or oil-packed), stemmed, seeded, and finely chopped, plus another small dried hot red pepper for serving (same prep)

1¼–1½ cups (200–250 grams) stale bread, crusts and all, torn into bite-size pieces

STUFFING

When I was a kid, Thanksgiving stuffing meant buying
loads of sliced Pepperidge Farm white bread and cutting it
into pieces and maybe letting them sit out overnight to dry
out a little. Maybe. And then mixing them with celery and
onions, maybe some sage, and stock made from the turkey
neck and giblets, and then shoving the stuffing inside the
turkey just before roasting. There might have been some
butter somewhere? It is all a little clouded in my memory,
but I remember loving it then.

Honestly, my approach now isn't all that wildly
different; it just relies on better ingredients, especially
when it comes to the bread. As with many other recipes
in this book, the older the bread, the better. When it is
completely dry, it can absorb a lot more liquid and flavor
while still retaining some texture and not mushing out.
A lot of bakeries around the holidays will sell bags of old
bread or bread cubes for stuffing. You can buy some from
your favorite bakery or start stockpiling old bread weeks
before the holiday. You can tear it for a more rugged
texture or cube it—whatever you prefer. Just make sure to
let it dry out completely before you make the stuffing.

The basic principles are going to be the same whether
you want to make a highly enriched, fancy stuffing or if
you want to keep it lean and classic. Amounts depend on
the size of your turkey and/or the number of people you
are feeding.

Instructions

Chop a few onions and a few sticks of celery. Cook them
in butter or in a mix of olive oil and butter, or even in
some rendered turkey fat, over medium-low heat until just
softened. Toss in a handful of sage leaves and a bay leaf or
a thyme sprig, if desired. Cook for about 10 minutes or so,
stirring until these aromatics are soft and smell good.

Toss in your pieces of old bread and stir to coat well with
the aromatics and the fat. Pour in enough stock or water to

almost cover the bread mixture and season with salt and pepper. Bring to a simmer, stirring occasionally, and cook until the bread begins to soften and the liquid is largely, but not totally, absorbed. You don't want the mixture too wet, nor do you want it too dry. Add more stock if it dries out early before the bread has softened. The amount of time this will take depends largely on how dry your bread is and how big the pieces are.

Allow to cool, then stir in a few beaten eggs. Loosely pack some of the stuffing inside your turkey and/or place it in a buttered baking dish, dotted with more butter and drizzled with a little more stock, as needed so the mixture is moist. Bake at whatever temperature you need your oven to be set at for the day, or until the top is golden brown and the stuffing registers 165°F on a probe thermometer. (Roughly an hour, more or less, at 400°F.)

If you prefer a more embellished stuffing, follow the same basic principles as above. If you want to add meat (sausage, bacon, pancetta, etc.), brown it first, render out any fat, remove with a slotted spoon, and then cook your onions, celery, and what have you in that fat with some additional butter if need be. Add the cooked meat back into the stuffing mixture before inserting it into the turkey or the baking dish.

Items such as mushrooms or chestnuts can be precooked in a separate pan first and added to the pot later.

CABBAGE AND POTATOES WITH BROKEN FRISELLE

Serves 4

This is a great recipe to use your friselle beyond just topping them with tomatoes in the summer. And who doesn't love cabbage and potatoes? For the latter, Yukon Gold or German butterball are nice. (If using German butterball, use a few more because they can be smaller.) The Calabrian sweet pepper powder adds a wonderful savory quality to the dish and is worth seeking out. If you can't find it, use the best-quality paprika you can find. Even Spanish pimentón could work here, but because it is smoked, go easy. It will take the dish in a different, but still enjoyable, direction.

Instructions

Place your potatoes in a large pot of well-salted water and bring to a boil. Meanwhile, remove the tough outer leaves of the cabbage, cut the cabbage in half, and discard the core. Roughly chop the cabbage. When the potatoes are barely fork-tender (start checking after 10 minutes), use a slotted spoon to transfer them to a large bowl of ice water to cool. Reserve the cooking water.

Immediately add the cabbage to the same pot and boil for 5 or 6 minutes, until softened. Use a slotted spoon to transfer it to the same bowl of ice water, reserving the cooking water. Drain and peel the potatoes, and set on a cutting board.

Lightly crush the garlic cloves with the heel of your hand or the flat side of a knife, leaving them whole with the skin still on. Place in a wide shallow pot, deep skillet, or sauté pan with the small hot peppers and a film of olive oil. If you want the dish a little spicier, you can break up one or both of the peppers into the oil.

INGREDIENTS

3–4 unpeeled yellow-fleshed medium potatoes, preferably of the same size (1–1¼ pounds; 450–600 grams total)

Salt

1 medium-to-large head of Savoy cabbage (1–2 pounds/500–1000 grams)

2–3 unpeeled garlic cloves

1–2 dried small red hot chile peppers

Olive oil

1 heaping tablespoon of Calabrian sweet red pepper powder or excellent-quality paprika

4–6 peperoni cruschi (optional; see page 102)

3–4 friselle, dried bread rusks, or pieces of dried bread (see Friselle, page 19)

Bring the heat up to medium and when the garlic and peppers start sizzling in the oil, add the spoonful of the Calabrian sweet pepper powder or paprika and a spoonful of the vegetable cooking water to prevent it from burning in the oil and becoming bitter. Stir. The mixture can burn quickly, so be mindful of this.

Drain the chopped cabbage from the bowl of ice water and add to the pot. Lightly salt and stir. Cook for a few minutes, stirring every so often, to flavor the cabbage and color it slightly. Slice the peeled potatoes and add to the pot. Don't worry about making perfect, nice slices. Irregularity is good here; just make them small enough to eat without having to cut in the dish. Season with a little salt and stir.

Taste the water you cooked the cabbage and potatoes in. If it isn't crazy salty, add a few ladles of it to the cabbage and potatoes. If it is too salty, just use fresh water—but you may need to add more salt to the dish. Add enough liquid to make it a little soupy, but not so much that the cabbage and potatoes are swimming. Cover and cook over low heat for a half hour or so, or until the cabbage and potatoes are very soft and the starch from the potatoes has thickened the liquid a little and everything in the pot has really gotten to know each other. Watch the water level and add a little more if you need it. Check for salt. Fish out and discard the garlic and hot peppers.

If using the peperoni cruschi, fry them in a film of hot oil until they darken and crisp up. Drain on paper towels.

Break up the friselle or dried bread among serving bowls. Ladle the cabbage and potatoes and their broth on top. Drizzle with some olive oil, top with the peperoni cruschi, if using, and serve hot.

Peperoni Cruschi

Peperoni cruschi (peperone crusco, singular) are dried red sweet peppers most commonly associated with Basilicata, but also used widely and enjoyed throughout mainland southern Italy in Calabria, Molise, Puglia, and parts of Abruzzo and Campania. Traditionally they are made from the Senise pepper, an elongated intensely flavored sweet pepper with thin flesh and low levels of moisture. After they are dried for storage, the stem and seeds are removed (although sometimes they are left whole for a more dramatic presentation), and they are fried quickly, preferably in olive oil, until they are crispy. They are often used to top certain pasta dishes, beans, pasta with beans, potatoes, eggs, a classic pairing with salt cod, a variety of different vegetable dishes, and so on. Or eaten on their own like potato chips. As such, they are great with many of the dishes in this book.

   Peperoni cruschi are very hard to find in the United States, but not impossible. We have included some sourcing options in the back of this book. Alternatively, you can dry your own sweet peppers to make them at home. Avoid bell peppers or any pepper that is too fleshy for this purpose. They will be a nightmare to dry and probably won't work out. Find thin-walled sweet peppers. I've had some luck in the past with drying Jimmy Nardello peppers. The taste is different, but you can achieve a somewhat similar effect. Peperoni di Senise seeds are available if you wanted to try and grow them yourself or if you wanted to beg and plead with a farmer in your community.

If you do go the route of ordering some peperoni cruschi, or someone happens to sell them near you, make sure that the package contains only the dried peppers and that they haven't already been fried. Once the peppers have been fried, they don't store particularly well, and they lose some of their taste and aroma and crunch.

To fry the dried peppers at home, fill a pan with enough olive oil to cover a few of the peppers at a time. Remove the stems and seeds from the peppers and if desired, tear them in half lengthwise. Heat the oil to around 350°F. Working in batches, fry a few peppers at a time until their color deepens and they puff a little. This happens fast, usually a few seconds. Remove from the oil with a slotted spoon or spider and drain on absorbent paper and lightly salt. This sounds incredibly easy and it is, but it takes some practice. Just a little too long in the oil and the peppers burn and become bitter and if they don't fry quite long enough, they won't be crispy after they cool and can have an unpleasant leathery chew. With a few tries you will dial it in the way you like it. Eat as is or use to top some of your favorite dishes.

MEATBALLS AND "MEATBALLS"

Doesn't everybody have four recipes for meatballs?
I could have included more. Meatballs are about bread,
not about meat—it's about using bread to stretch your
ingredients.

POLPETTI DI PANE, OR BREAD "MEATBALLS"

Serves 2 to 4 (makes about 20)

I first encountered bread "meatballs" in a modest restaurant in Reggio Calabria. Like almost every restaurant in the area, signs outside promised antichi sapori—"ancient flavors"—and prodotti tipici—local, literally "typical," products. It served a few unadorned fried polpetti as antipasti alongside some local Pecorino, a few slices of cured meat, some marinated vegetables, and a wedge of onion frittata. The restaurant was actually not particularly good or memorable, but the bread meatballs have stayed with me.

Some cooks like to add dried currants and pine nuts or almonds to their polpetti, and that can be nice, though I prefer the beautiful simplicity of them without. Additionally, some cooks flatten the bread mixture into small patties before frying instead of rolling them into balls. This allows you to fry them in less oil. The texture ends up slightly different, but either method produces good results.

INGREDIENTS

1 large slice (150 grams) stale bread in pieces (preferably without the crust)

1¾ cups (400 ml) whole milk (or as needed, depending on just how dry your bread is)

4 ounces (one 125-gram chunk) hard Pecorino

Handful fresh flat-leaf parsley leaves

1 small garlic clove

1 egg

Salt

Freshly ground black pepper

Olive oil for frying

Instructions

Place the pieces of bread in a mixing bowl. If any of the pieces are particularly large, break them up so you have smaller pieces more or less uniform in size (about an inch across).

Heat the milk in a pan until it is hot but not boiling, stirring occasionally to prevent it from forming a skin. Pour the hot milk over the bread in the bowl. Stir every now and then to make sure all the pieces are submerged, allowing them to absorb the liquid evenly.

Meanwhile, grate the cheese, finely chop the parsley, and mince the garlic. Use a fork to beat the egg thoroughly in a bowl. →

After the bread has absorbed all the milk, give it a squeeze. The pieces should be soft but not excessively wet. If they aren't entirely soft and there isn't any milk left in the bowl, heat a little more milk and add it to the mixture. If the bread has softened, but it weeps when you squeeze it, drain in a sieve before you proceed.

Add the cheese, parsley, garlic, and egg to the softened bread mixture. Season with salt and pepper and knead thoroughly in the bowl until you have a homogeneous mixture.

With slightly damp hands, roll the mixture into balls slightly smaller than ping-pong balls (about 1¼ inches in diameter) and place on a lightly greased sheet pan or a plate (or you can place them on a sheet pan lined with paper towels to absorb excess moisture).

Line a plate with paper towels. Heat a few inches of oil in a small pot. Once the oil is hot (350°–360°F) but not smoking, deep-fry the bread balls in batches of three or four until they are golden brown—2½ to 3 minutes—and transfer them to the paper towels to drain. The polpetti will firm up as they cool. Wait a minute or two for the oil to come back to temperature in between batches.

At this point, you can either serve them as is or simmer them briefly in Quick Tomato Sauce (page 114) before serving.

MEATBALLS

Serves 2 to 4 (makes about 20)

These are the meatballs people most often ask for at my shop. The distinction between what I'm doing and what others do: Most people don't use this much bread. The Italian American approach tends to be pouring bread crumbs into a meat mixture. I generally use at least 30 percent bread to meat. Drier bread weighs less than bread that has moisture left inside, so if your bread is on the dry side, you'll need more.

INGREDIENTS

A little more than ½ cup (at least 135 grams) stale bread torn into pieces (it should be 2 or 3 days old, soft interior, no crust, starting to dry out but still with a little bit of give)

2¾ cups (650 ml) milk or water—enough to moisten the bread; drier bread needs more liquid

2¼ cups (450 grams) ground beef

¼ cup (60 grams) grated aged Pecorino

1 tablespoon (20 grams) grated Parmigiano

A handful or so of fresh flat-leaf parsley, stemmed and finely chopped

1–2 eggs

1 clove garlic, minced

Salt

Pepper

Olive or grapeseed oil for frying

Instructions

First, tear the bread into small pieces. Heat the milk or water until it's warm but not boiling, and pour it on the bread on a rimmed sheet pan. Let it sit until the bread absorbs most of the milk and the mixture cools enough to easily handle.

Once the bread has absorbed the milk, squeeze out the milk like a sponge; you have to drain it really thoroughly to avoid excess liquid that would get into the meatballs. Then add bread to the ground beef and work it into a paste. Next, add the grated cheeses, parsley, egg, garlic, salt, and pepper, and mix thoroughly with your hands.

Once you have mixed it really well and it's all bound in a homogeneous mixture, pinch off a nugget and cook in a skillet over medium-high heat and taste to see if it's seasoned well. Adjust seasoning as needed.

Form the meatball mixture into balls the size of ping-pong balls (about 1¼ inches in diameter). Dampen your palm and roll, with joined fingers on one hand, and slightly cupped on the other. Roll them very gently; have a little bowl of water next to you to keep your palm damp, but not wet. You want nice, smooth surfaces on your meatball. When they're too dry, they crack; then when you fry them, they take on more oil and come apart. →

Once the meatballs have been shaped, allow them to rest in the fridge for a while, from an hour to overnight (but if you do overnight the meat will oxidize a bit).

When you're ready to cook them, heat enough oil to cover the meatballs to 350°F in a deep pot. Fry in batches for about 2 to 3 minutes, using two forks to turn them very gently as they cook. They should be brown and crisp on the outside and soft on the inside.

Allow the oil to come back up to temperature before adding the next batch. Use a slotted spoon to transfer the meatballs to paper towels to drain. Serve with Quick Tomato Sauce (page 114).

113

QUICK TOMATO SAUCE

Makes about 2½ cups

I like to use Gustarosso brand canned tomatoes here, available at Gustiamo.com (see Essential Ingredients, page xxvii). Use a tomato brand that speaks to you.

Instructions

Lightly coat a sauté pan with olive oil. Add the garlic and start the heat on low, increasing it gradually so the garlic has time to release its flavor without burning.

Once the garlic begins to sizzle, add the chile pepper and some of the liquid from the canned tomatoes. Crush the tomatoes by hand into the pan, season with salt, and toss in the basil. Increase the heat to medium-high, partially cover, and cook for 6 to 8 minutes, until the chunks of tomato have mostly broken down to form a reduced and thickened sauce.

INGREDIENTS

Olive oil

1 small garlic clove, thinly sliced

1 small hot red chile pepper (dried or fresh), stemmed, seeded, and finely chopped

One 28-ounce can (about 3 cups/360 grams) top-quality canned whole, peeled tomatoes with their juices

Salt

1–2 fresh basil leaves

POLPETTI DI BOLLITO, OR BOILED BEEF MEATBALLS

Makes 30 to 40

I first encountered boiled beef meatballs in Rome on my first visit to Gabriele Bonci's remarkable Pizzarium. Though it would be tragic to visit Pizzarium and eat too many suppli or polpetti and diminish your appetite for pizza, they're great and worth it. Or you can make them at home. This recipe feeds a party.

Historically this is the way one would use the meat left over after making a broth, or leftover boiled meat.

INGREDIENTS

For the beef

Salt

1 peeled large yellow onion, studded with a few whole cloves

2 carrots, scrubbed well and cut in half

1 celery rib, cut in half

1 bay leaf

A few sprigs fresh flat-leaf parsley

A few whole black peppercorns (optional)

About 3½ pounds (1.75 kilograms) beef brisket, shoulder, or shank (does not need to be trimmed)

For the meatballs

1 cup (200 grams) old crustless bread, dried out yet still retaining a little give to the crumb

1¾ cups (420 ml) milk

¾ cup (100 grams) mortadella, finely chopped

2 medium potatoes (350 grams), peeled, boiled, and coarsely mashed (2 cups)

1 bunch fresh flat-leaf parsley, stemmed and finely chopped

1 garlic clove, minced →

Instructions

For the beef: Add enough water to a large pot to eventually cover the meat and the vegetables. Lightly salt the water, then add the onion, carrots, celery, bay leaf, parsley, and peppercorns, if using, and bring to a boil. Add the meat and reduce the heat to a simmer, skimming off any foam. The meat and vegetables should be submerged; add water as needed. Cook, uncovered, until the meat is tender enough to be shredded with a fork—2 hours or more, depending on the cut and how low your burner will go. (Keep skimming as needed.) Remove from the heat, discard the vegetables and aromatics, and let the meat cool a little in the broth.

For the meatballs: Place the bread in a heatproof bowl. Heat the milk in a saucepan until warm but not boiling, then pour it over the bread. Allow the bread to soak up as much of the milk as it can while periodically, using a wooden spoon or your hands, breaking up the pieces as they soften.

When the meat is still warm but cool enough to handle, transfer it to a large mixing bowl. Use a fork or your hands to coarsely shred it. Discard the broth. Mix in the mortadella and mashed potatoes. Pulse half of the →

meat/potato mixture in a food processor in small batches until finely chopped, then return it to the large bowl with the rest of the meat. It will clump together and look lighter in color.

Add the parsley, garlic, cheeses, eggs, and lemon zest. Squeeze out any excess milk from the bread, then add the drained bread to the mixture in the large bowl. Season with salt, pepper, and a few gratings of nutmeg (a little of the last goes a long way). Mix thoroughly by hand until well combined. Taste for seasoning and adjust as needed.

For the meatballs: Heat the oil to 350°F in a deep pot.

Place the flour, beaten eggs, and bread crumbs in separate dishes. Form the meatball mixture into balls the size of ping-pong balls (about 1¼ inches in diameter) or patties 2½ to 3 inches by about ¾ inch thick, or into torpedo shapes about 3 inches long and 1½ inches wide. Roll in flour to coat evenly, dip in the beaten eggs, then place in the bread crumbs. Roll to coat evenly, being careful to preserve the shape of the soft meatball. Shake off any excess crumbs. Fry in batches for about 2 to 3 minutes, or until golden brown and crisp all over, using two forks to turn them and allowing the oil to come back up to temperature before adding the next batch. Use a slotted spoon to transfer the meatballs to a plate lined with paper towels to drain.

Serve with lemon wedges, if desired.

About ¾ cup (75 grams) Parmigiano Reggiano cheese, finely grated

About ¾ cup (75 grams) aged Pecorino, finely grated

3 eggs, beaten

Freshly grated zest of 1 lemon

Salt

Freshly ground black pepper

Freshly grated nutmeg

For assembly

Oil for frying

Flour

Eggs, beaten

2¼–3 cups (225–300 grams) finely ground Toasted Bread Crumbs (page 125)

Lemon wedges for serving (optional)

RICOTTA "MEATBALLS"

Makes 26 to 30

There is no meat in these meatballs, but calling them "dumplings" (the English translation of "polpette") feels odd to me.

Ricotta means "recooked," and is a cheese made from the whey left over from the process of making another cheese. Italian ricotta is lighter in texture and more delicate in taste than the whole-milk or part-skim ricotta found in most grocery stores in the United States. I use Caputo Brothers Creamery ricotta, and, as far as I know, it is one of the few examples of traditional whey-based ricotta commercially available. Another option would be to make friends with cheesemakers near you and convince them to start making traditional whey-based ricotta. If they work with sheep or goats, all the better for you. (They need to do something with all of the whey, and pigs can only eat so much.) If whole-milk or part-skim ricotta is your only option, you can still make these, but know that better options are out there for you.

These are cooked in a simple tomato sauce, but if you prefer, you can poach them in homemade chicken broth and enjoy them in a soup, or roll the ricotta balls in flour, beaten egg, then bread crumbs. Fry them and eat as is.

INGREDIENTS

¾ packed cup (85 grams) stale bread, crusts removed

1 cup (200 ml) whole milk

1 packed cup (250 grams) ricotta cheese

1 egg

¼–⅓ cup (20–30 grams) grated aged Pecorino

Leaves from a few sprigs fresh flat-leaf parsley, finely chopped

3 cups (300 grams) finely ground Toasted Bread Crumbs (page 125)

Salt

Oil for tray or sheet pan

1–2 cups (235 to 475 ml) Quick Tomato Sauce (page 114) or other simple tomato sauce

Instructions

Tear up the bread in a bowl. Heat the milk in a small pan until hot but not boiling, then pour over the bread, pressing it down to make sure the bread absorbs as much of the milk as possible.

In a separate bowl, mix the ricotta, egg, Pecorino to taste, and parsley.

When the bread has softened and absorbed all or at least most of the milk and is completely cool, squeeze out and discard any excess milk. Add the soaked bread to the ricotta mixture and combine. If the mixture is too soft →

and wet, add some fine bread crumbs, just a little at a time, until it firms up a little. You don't want the mixture so wet that it is too hard to roll into balls, but you don't want it particularly stiff, either. The softer it is, the lighter the final product will be. The added bread crumbs will absorb excess liquid and make them easier to handle, but they also will make the final product a little drier and potentially heavier. Practice will help you get the texture just right.

Season with salt to taste. Cover and let the mixture rest in the refrigerator for about 1 hour. Time in the cold will firm up the mixture a little, so keep that in mind before or while you are adding bread crumbs. The chilled mixture should hold together well.

Lightly grease a tray or sheet pan with oil. Place a small bowl of water nearby to keep your hands damp. Roll the ricotta mixture into 26 to 30 small balls 1 to 1½ inches in diameter and place them on the tray until you are ready to cook them.

Working in batches as needed, poach the ricotta balls in the tomato sauce (at a low simmer) for 10 to 12 minutes, or until cooked through. They will plump up and feel firmer to the touch.

Serve warm.

MBS

I cannot emphasize enough the difference between buying bad bread crumbs, buying good bread crumbs, and making your own. The difference in texture and flavor is significant. If you're committed to spending good money on good bread, you should plan on making your own bread crumbs. And if you don't make your own, buy them only from the artisan bakery where you're buying bread. Make them weeks ahead or as you're preparing dinner.

Because they are one of the simplest and most useful ingredients in any kitchen, bread crumbs can serve as the foundation for so many recipes.

Basically, you're reducing large pieces of bread into smaller pieces. The best way to do this depends on the characteristics of the bread you're using, and the type and amount of bread crumbs required.

For the purposes of these recipes, we'll be using bread crumbs that in Italian are called pangrattato, and are made from thoroughly dried-out bread.

BASIC BREAD CRUMBS

For frying in particular

If your bread is not terribly old and still has a little life left in the crumb, grate it on the large-holed side of a box grater set over a bowl. This method provides a nice light, varied texture. Grating bread on a microplane can also work if the bread has some yield or softness and is not completely dried out. It can produce relatively small amounts of very fine bread crumbs that are suitable for coating foods before frying.

If your bread is quite hard, break or cut it into chunks and pulse them in the food processor until they are reduced to the consistency you desire. But make sure that you are working in batches; put in a small amount and remove it all once it's processed—as opposed to adding more chunks as the crumbs reduce, which can lead to unevenly sized crumbs. This method is faster than using a box grater and works well for processing lots of bread crumbs. A blender can do the job as well.

If your bread is completely dry, crush it in a mortar and pestle or place it inside a cloth bag (thick plastic bags can work, but are prone to tearing) and smash it with a rolling pin, meat tenderizer, or any blunt object of your choosing.

You can sift the bread crumbs through a mesh sieve to obtain crumbs of varying levels of fineness for different purposes.

TOASTED BREAD CRUMBS

For topping pasta or other cooked dishes

Instructions

Preheat the oven to 350°F.

INGREDIENTS

A quarter loaf, half loaf, or any variation on chunks of bread, reduced to crumbs using one of the methods on page 124

Olive oil

Spread the bread crumbs across a rimmed baking sheet in a single layer. Drizzle with just enough oil to barely coat the crumbs evenly, tossing them to achieve a texture that's closer to dry than damp.

Bake for a few minutes, then give the crumbs a stir to promote even browning. Continue baking; once the bread crumbs turn an attractive shade of reddish brown—watch them closely, 5 to 10 minutes—slide them onto a plate to stop their cooking.

Alternatively, heat a cast-iron or nonstick skillet over medium heat. Once the pan is hot, pour in a thin coat of oil and add the bread crumbs. Stir frequently until the crumbs are the desired color. Transfer them to a plate lined with a paper towel to drain and cool.

Store the cooled toasted bread crumbs in an airtight container, and use them as needed. They'll last forever—or at least a few months.

PASTA

Everybody associates Italy with pasta and the consumption of pasta, but that's pretty much a modern phenomenon. Up until the late nineteenth and early twentieth centuries, people didn't eat pasta the way they do now. It was bread that took that role in every meal, and that's still very visible today.

Pasta and bread should be seen as two sides of the same coin, because they're both ways of preserving wheat. Here's an agricultural product that has a shelf life, so what can you do to make it edible? Then, once we've made wheat into flour, how are we going to ensure that it keeps? One way is to make pasta, which is a very shelf-stable product.

I realize that it takes a little extra legwork to find it, but consider buying pasta brands like Benedetto Cavalieri or Faella, crafted according to tradition in the birthplace of Italian dried pasta, Gragnano. These companies, which have been around for more than 100 years, use better varietals of (usually) durum wheat. And they've perfected the craft of making and drying pasta, leading to a product that has a sweet nutty scent, like bread while it's baking. In addition, the texture is more substantive, maybe a little chewy in a good way. And better pasta is more porous, which allows sauces to coat the noodles. You may be paying $10 a bag. But that bag feeds four to six people—are the people you're feeding worth $2.50 a plate? I hope so, especially for pastas that taste as good as these do.

A few random pasta notes: Cook pasta al dente and don't be afraid to cook it risotto-style when the situation calls for it—like that Romanesco recipe on page 136. Save your pasta water, and when you're introducing it into a dish for a sauce, be sure to add it a splash at a time so it doesn't make things too watery and you're allowing time for the liquid to coat the noodles.

And while I have just a handful of recipes here in which bread crumbs are added to pasta, really, the possibilities are endless.

PASTA WITH BREAD CRUMBS AND RAISINS

Serves 2

Savory, sweet, spicy, oily, crunchy: this Sicilian recipe is simple and minimalist, but the raisins add an element of sweetness.

Instructions

Bring a large pot of water to a boil. Salt it generously. Ladle about ¼ cup of that hot water over the raisins in a bowl to rehydrate and soften them. Add the pasta to the pot of boiling salted water.

Meanwhile, thinly slice the garlic. Finely chop the hot pepper. Add the garlic to a skillet with a thread of olive oil and start over low heat. Once the garlic begins to sizzle, stir in the chopped hot pepper, then dump in the raisins with their soaking liquid.

Once the spaghetti is almost cooked, drain it, reserving some of the cooking water. Add the noodles to the skillet; increase the heat to high and toss it with the raisins, adding pasta cooking water as needed, until it is cooked al dente. Check for salt. Drizzle in a little olive oil, toss with the toasted bread crumbs, and add a few leaves of parsley, if desired. Serve with additional bread crumbs at the table.

INGREDIENTS

Salt

2 tablespoons (20 grams) golden raisins

3½ ounces (100 grams) dried spaghetti

1 garlic clove

1 small dried hot chile pepper, stemmed and seeded

Olive oil

1½ cups (250 grams) Toasted Bread Crumbs, plus more for serving (see page 125)

Fresh flat-leaf parsley (optional)

Raisins

Seek out good raisins. Not all of them are created equal. In fact, a lot of raisins are manufactured through completely industrial processes and contain added preservatives and extra sugar. Other raisins are made through a slower and more natural (also more expensive, but worth it) process. Good raisins are dried outside in the sun (or in some cases the shade) on mats or trays. This only works in places and times without a lot of humidity and that have the right kinds of climates.

Zibibbo raisins from Sicily are incredibly good. They still contain their seeds, which are edible, but you can remove them if you dislike the texture. I kind of like it. Raisins from Herat in western Afghanistan are also wonderful, though they have a completely different flavor and color than the Zibibbo raisins. They are a little sweeter and are greenish in color. If you are lucky, you can sometimes find these in some international markets. (See Resources, page 225.)

A note on buying raisins: You want to use the best, but realistically those are harder to find unless you get them by special order. Otherwise, look for raisins that are organic, which are going to be more dried out and less plump than most raisins that are treated with preservatives and boiled in sugar water. If the raisins you find have more than one ingredient listed, I encourage you not to buy them. Keep looking.

PASTA WITH BREAD CRUMBS AND ANCHOVIES

Serves 2 to 3

INGREDIENTS

1 garlic clove

2 whole salted anchovies

1 tablespoon (15 grams) salted capers

12 oil-cured black olives

A few sprigs fresh flat-leaf parsley (optional)

Salt

9 ounces (250 grams) dried spaghetti

Olive oil

1 small dried red hot chile pepper, chopped, seeds removed (chile flakes will work in a pinch)

2 cups (200 grams) Toasted Bread Crumbs, plus extra for the table (page 125)

In southern Italy, many pasta dishes are topped with toasted bread crumbs instead of or in addition to grated cheese. The prevailing logic dictates that in some households, when they couldn't afford cheese or wanted to stretch what cheese they had, they would use bread crumbs instead.

No matter how much money you have, bread crumbs on pasta are great. They provide a texture cheese only wishes it had.

Instructions

Bring a large pot of water to a boil. Smash the clove of garlic with the heel of your hand (or the flat side of your knife if you are more that type of person).

Rinse the salted anchovies under running water (page xxxi). Use your thumb to gently open the cavity of the anchovies and rinse away the salt inside the fish and any remaining guts. Remove the spines and fins, separate the fillets, and let dry on paper towels.

Rinse the capers under running water, then soak in fresh water in a small bowl.

Pit the olives. Finely chop the parsley, if using.

When the water comes to a raging boil, salt heavily but judiciously and drop in the pasta. (I always salt the water for pasta very generously, so it tastes like the sea, unless the sauce for the pasta utilizes a lot of naturally salty ingredients, like this dish does. Then I cut back a bit.)

Coat the bottom of a skillet with a film of olive oil, toss in the smashed garlic clove and the hot pepper, and set on a medium heat. When the garlic begins to sizzle and →

turns golden (in approximately a minute), add the anchovies, capers, and olives. Add a splash of pasta water and stir to dissolve the anchovies. Take the pan off the heat and remove the garlic clove and the hot pepper.

When the pasta is still slightly firmer than you would like to eat it, drain it in a colander, making sure to reserve some of the pasta water. Turn up the heat under the skillet and add the pasta. Add a half ladle of the reserved pasta water and cook, tossing the pasta with the other ingredients while the water boils away (you don't want this to be very wet). When the water is gone, and the pasta is cooked al dente (ideally this will happen at the same time), turn off the heat, add the toasted bread crumbs, a little olive oil, and the parsley, if using, and toss thoroughly to coat the strands of spaghetti. Serve with more bread crumbs at the table if desired.

PASTA WITH BREAD CRUMBS AND CAULIFLOWER

Serves 2 to 3

Instructions

Bring a large pot of water to a rolling boil. Salt it generously. Add the cauliflower and cook for 5 to 6 minutes, or until tender. Use a slotted spoon to transfer it to a bowl, along with a few tablespoons of the cooking water. Once the pot returns to a boil, add the pasta.

Meanwhile, thinly slice only the white part of the spring onion. Place in a skillet with some olive oil and bring the heat up slowly, to medium. Cook the onions until soft and sweet, but not colored, about 5 minutes. Drain the raisins, then stir them and the pine nuts into the skillet. Cook for a minute or two, then add the tomato paste. Add the cooked cauliflower and a few spoonfuls of the cooking water. Mix well to dissolve the tomato paste and mash up most of the cauliflower with a wooden spoon.

Just before the pasta is cooked to al dente, use a slotted spoon to transfer it to the skillet. Increase the heat to high and toss with the cauliflower sauce to coat well, and give it a few more minutes to finish cooking. Add a little of the cooking water as needed to aid in this process. The final dish should be dry and not too saucy, with the cauliflower and the pine nuts clinging to the pasta.

Remove from the heat, check for salt, season with the pepper, and give it a light thread of olive oil. Top with the bread crumbs and serve. If you are a little underwhelmed by the color of the final dish, a few leaves of parsley can help.

INGREDIENTS

Salt

1 small head of cauliflower
(1 pound/450 grams), trimmed
and separated into large florets

7 ounces (about 2 cups/200 grams)
dried short pasta such as
ziti or casarecce

1 spring onion, root end trimmed

Olive oil

2 tablespoons (25 grams)
golden raisins

2 tablespoons (25 grams) pine nuts

Small spoonful of tomato paste (strattu)

Freshly ground black pepper

¾–1 cup (75–100 grams) Toasted
Bread Crumbs (page 125)

Fresh flat-leaf parsley leaves (optional)

Pine nuts

The majority of pine nuts available in American grocery stores are grown in Russia, Siberia, and North Korea and are processed in China. And they are terrible. I am not sure I have ever encountered a Chinese pine nut in the U.S. that wasn't rancid. Many people recognize this as the flavor of pine nuts.

There is even a condition known as "pine nut mouth" that comes from eating bad pine nuts, and leaves a bitter, metallic taste behind and can change the eater's taste for all food for days. Fresh, quality pine nuts are wonderful, but they're expensive and hard to find.

The labor involved in harvesting and processing pine nuts is intense. Some international markets sell pine nuts that have been removed from the pine cones but are still in their shell. If you can find these, you should buy them, because an afternoon spent performing the difficult task of shelling just a small handful of nuts will give you a newfound appreciation and understanding of the ingredient.

Seek out Mediterranean pine nuts if you can. They are long and slender compared to the more common Chinese pine nut, and generally taste better. The types of pine that produce pine nuts actually grow well in many parts of the United States but can take around fifteen years from planting until the first harvest. Some young American farmers need to get on this. They'll make really good money. Eventually.

If Mediterranean pine nuts are not available where you live and you don't want to order them through the internet or don't feel like spending the money on them, substitute other kinds of nuts. I have used almonds or walnuts with great success. That said, when purchasing any nut, seek out new-crop nuts and buy them from someone who can at least tell you where they came from and when they were harvested.

PASTA WITH ROMANESCO CAULIFLOWER, ANCHOVIES, AND BREAD CRUMBS

Serves 2 to 4

Although it is not always the preferred method, I like to cook this and some other pastas in the style of risotto. The cauliflower almost completely breaks down to a sauce, and the starch from the pasta makes it extra silky and creamy if you get it just right. It is a great method to learn if you are ever in a situation where you only have one burner. The bread crumbs add some welcome texture to pasta cooked in this fashion.

Instructions

Trim the cauliflower head, then cut it into very small florets or pieces.

Bring 4 cups of water to a boil, then lightly salt. (You may not use all of it.)

Add a pour of olive oil to a wide pan and put in the sliced garlic. Break up the hot red pepper into the oil (or add the crushed hot red pepper).

Turn the heat up to medium. As soon as the garlic begins sizzling, add the anchovy fillets and stir to dissolve them in the hot oil. Do not let the garlic brown or the anchovies burn. A spoonful of water can help if it looks like it is getting away from you.

Add the cauliflower to the anchovies and garlic, stir well and cover. Let the cauliflower steam in the flavored oil, adding a spoonful of water from time to time if absolutely necessary to prevent it from browning. Lightly salt and stir periodically, mashing some of the cauliflower with a wooden spoon in the pan as it softens. →

INGREDIENTS

1 small to medium head Romanesco cauliflower (about 1 pound/300–500 grams)

Salt

Olive oil

1 garlic clove, thinly sliced

1 small dried hot red chile pepper, or some crushed hot red pepper, if you must

2–4 anchovy fillets, preferably salted and rinsed (see page xxxi)

Generous 2 cups (200 grams) short dried pasta such as mezze maniche, rigatoni, maccheroni, or even pasta mista (a mix of a bunch of different shapes and broken pieces of pasta)

1 cup grated aged Pecorino (or 100-gram chunk)

1 cup (100 grams) medium to coarsely ground Toasted Bread Crumbs (page 125)

When the cauliflower is soft and fully cooked (about 20 minutes), uncover and add the pasta, stirring well to coat. Turn up the heat and continue stirring. As soon as the pasta begins to stick a little, add a ladle full of water to loosen, stirring and scraping the pan. Continue to stir and give the pan an occasional toss, adding water a little at a time as the pasta absorbs it. The mixture should be wet enough to stay fluid in the pan, but not so wet as to be brothy. The pasta should actually cook and release its starch, with not a lot of liquid in the pan once it is cooked to your liking—and certainly not so dry as to make the dish stodgy.

Shortly before the pasta is al dente, turn off the heat. Grate in some Pecorino and add a drizzle of oil and taste for salt. Splash in a little more water if necessary and let the pasta rest a minute or two, covered, to finish cooking in the residual heat from the pan. Serve, topped with a little more cheese and a generous scattering of toasted bread crumbs.

PASTA ALLA PAOLINA

Serves 2

Judicious spicing with cloves and cinnamon gives this Sicilian pasta dish its Middle Eastern flavors. It was allegedly invented by a Sicilian monk at the Monastery San Francesco di Paola in Palermo.

INGREDIENTS

Salt

3 whole salted anchovies

1 small garlic clove

2–3 whole cloves

One 3-inch cinnamon stick

7 ounces (200 grams) dried bucatini or ziti

Olive oil

1 cup (225 grams) canned whole tomatoes

Finely ground Toasted Bread Crumbs, if needed for thickening (page 125)

A few fresh basil leaves

Freshly ground black pepper

Instructions

Bring a large pot of water to a rolling boil. Salt it generously.

In the meantime, rinse the anchovies well. Split them open with your thumb and discard their spines and fins. Place in a bowl and use a fork to mash them to a paste or finely chop them. Mince the garlic. Pound the cloves (whether you use 2 or 3 depends on your personal preference) in a mortar and pestle or in a spice grinder and finely grate a little cinnamon on a microplane into a small bowl (just a few passes, you don't need a ton).

Add the pasta to the boiling water.

Add the minced garlic and olive oil to a skillet and bring up the heat slowly to medium. Once the garlic begins to sizzle and becomes fragrant, add the mashed anchovies and stir. Crush the tomatoes by hand into the skillet. Lightly season with salt and add the grated cinnamon and freshly ground cloves. Cook and reduce the sauce, stirring occasionally, while the pasta is cooking.

Just before the pasta is cooked to al dente, use tongs or a slotted spoon to transfer it from the pot to the skillet, tossing to coat it well with the sauce, and finish cooking. Add a few tablespoons of cooking water to loosen the sauce, as needed. If your sauce is too loose, add some of the toasted bread crumbs to thicken it.

Remove from the heat, check for salt. Add a few torn basil leaves and a light thread of olive oil. Season generously with the pepper.

PASTA WITH PIENNOLO TOMATOES AND BREAD CRUMBS

Serves 2

The Piennolo tomato is less famous than the San Marzano, its relative and neighbor. Both are grown in the volcanic soil of Campania around Mount Vesuvius. The Piennolo is smaller, sweeter, and less common in the United States. Slightly elongated, with a pronounced "nipple" at the end, Piennolo tomatoes are interesting because of their incredible flavor, but also because of how they are hung in large bunches and stored for a long time.

Farmers in the United States are beginning to grow this cherry tomato varietal, which is worth seeking out and cooking with—though I suspect that those tomatoes will never be quite the same as the ones grown near Vesuvius.

Colatura (di Alici) is a relative of the ancient Roman fish sauce known as garum. It is made in Cetara, outside Naples, and is collected in the process of making salted anchovies. It is subtle compared to many Southeast Asian–style fish sauces but delivers a wonderful depth of flavor to any dish you use it in.

Typically, I suggest salting the water aggressively when making pasta. In this case, it is better to go easy. The anchovy, capers, and colatura all deliver salinity; better to under-salt, and correct at the end as needed.

INGREDIENTS

Salt

12 yellow Piennolo tomatoes or sweet yellow cherry tomatoes, fresh or jarred

1 garlic clove

20 salted capers, rinsed well and drained

1 whole salted anchovy (see Resources, page 225)

Olive oil

4 ounces (about 115 grams) dried linguine (I make a lot)

Smidgen dried chile pepper flakes

Colatura (optional)

A few leaves fresh flat-leaf parsley for garnish

1 cup (100 grams) Toasted Bread Crumbs (page 125)

Instructions

Bring a large pot of water to a rolling boil, then salt it generously. If you wish to skin the fresh tomatoes (it's more rustic to leave them on), fill a large bowl with water and ice cubes and score a shallow X through the stem end of each tomato, drop into the boiling water for 30 seconds, then use a slotted spoon to immediately transfer them to the ice water bath. Drain when cool, and discard the skins.

Thinly slice the garlic. Rinse the capers in a colander and soak in a small bowl of cold water. Clean and rinse the salted anchovy.

Coat a wide skillet with a thin film of oil. Add the garlic and start the heat on medium-low.

Meanwhile, drop the pasta into the boiling pot.

Once the garlic begins to sizzle, add the dried red pepper flakes, anchovy fillet, and drained capers. Stir and cook for a minute, breaking up the fillet.

Add the tomatoes and 2 or 3 tablespoons of the pasta cooking water to the skillet, then increase the heat to high. Shake and stir the pan often, crushing a few of the tomatoes with a wooden spoon to release their juices. Add more of that pasta water a little at a time as needed, to prevent sticking. You don't want the sauce to stick, but it shouldn't be too wet and loose. The tomatoes should begin to collapse but not entirely fall apart.

Before the linguine is cooked to al dente, use tongs to transfer it straight from the boiling water to the skillet. Add a little more pasta cooking water, judiciously and vigorously tossing and stirring over high heat to finish the cooking of the pasta. Getting the starch to emulsify with the scant sauce is key here to making this pasta (and most pasta dishes) great.

Once the pasta is just shy of perfectly cooked, turn off the heat. Always remember: it will continue to cook in residual heat just a little. (You don't want to cook pasta absolutely perfectly and then have it a little softer than you would like by the time you bring it to the table.) Add a splash of colatura to the pasta, if using, the parsley, and a drizzle of oil, and toss.

Top with toasted bread crumbs and serve.

GNOCCHI DI PANE,
OR BREAD GNOCCHI

Serves 2 to 4

Gnocchi are tricky. Handle the dough too much, and they become dense, leaden lumps that sit heavy in the stomach. Handle it too little, and they can fall apart in the cooking water. Making great gnocchi is largely about feel more than it is about any recipe, and it might take some practice to get it right.

Bread gnocchi are from northern Italy and are comparatively easy to handle. A few of them in a butter-sage sauce make a great first course for a hearty winter meal.

Instructions

For the gnocchi: Heat the milk until just below simmering and pour over the bread crumbs in a bowl. Allow the bread crumbs to fully rehydrate and soften in the milk for about 10 minutes.

Vigorously whisk the egg in a separate bowl. Grate the cheese (about ½ cup) into the egg, using the fine holes on a box grater. Squeeze out any excess milk from the bread crumbs using your hands. (There might not be excess milk; it depends on how old your bread crumbs are.) Add the egg and the grated cheese to the bread crumbs. Season with salt and pepper and the faintest whisper of nutmeg, if desired.

Mix gently while sifting in the flour a little at a time. You want to use the absolute minimum of flour needed to help bind the gnocchi, and make sure you are handling the mixture as gently as possible to achieve the lightest possible texture. Not so gently, however, that they fall apart when they hit the boiling water.

Bring a large pot of water to a rolling boil, then salt it generously.

INGREDIENTS

For the gnocchi

2 cups (450 ml) milk

1½ cups plus 2 tablespoons (about 165 grams) Basic Bread Crumbs (page 124)

1 egg

One 1.75-ounce (50-gram) chunk of Parmigiano Reggiano, plus more grated for serving

Salt

Freshly ground black pepper

Freshly grated nutmeg (optional)

5 tablespoons plus 1 teaspoon (50 grams) flour, or as needed

For serving

8 tablespoons (113 grams) of the best-quality butter you can find, salted or unsalted

Small handful fresh sage leaves

Once the gnocchi mixture is pretty homogeneous, gently form a quarter-size or golf-ball-size ball, depending on your preference, by rolling a small clump of the mixture in the damp, cupped palm of your hand. Lightly roll the ball across a gnocchi paddle or the tines of a fork. Test a gnocco by gently dropping it in the boiling water to see whether it holds its shape. If it does, you are good to go. Remove it when it begins to rise to the surface of the water. Taste for seasoning, and adjust the remaining gnocchi mixture as needed.

If the gnocco fell apart, mix in a little more flour. Test again until you get it to work. When you know your mixture is good, finish shaping the gnocchi, placing them on a floured baking sheet as you go. You should be able to get about 30 gnocchi (including testers). Place the baking sheet with the gnocchi, uncovered, in the refrigerator until you are ready to cook them (try to cook them within a day). This will help dry them out a little, which is good—when they're a little drier, they'll more easily keep their shape.

When you're ready to serve, bring your salted water back to a boil.

Meanwhile, melt the butter in a sauté pan over medium heat until it just begins to brown. Toss in the sage leaves, then remove the pan from the heat. Working in batches, drop your gnocchi in the boiling water. When they begin to float, after a few minutes, use a slotted spoon to transfer them to the melted butter and sage in the pan, along with a splash of the gnocchi cooking water. Toss gently to coat the gnocchi (gently reheating if necessary). Serve in shallow bowls topped with grated Parmigiano.

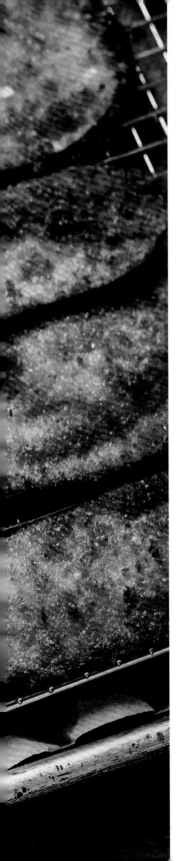

FRIED THINGS

We don't celebrate fried things enough. The Italians? They've got their own fry shops—like a friggitoria in Naples, where you can get any manner of fried things. Little minnow-like fried fish in a cone. Pizza fritta. Croquettes. Polenta. Eggplant. Zucchini blossoms. Of course, you'd find arancini and suppli—some of my favorite recipes in this book (and a delicious thing to eat before moving on to pizza). I can go on and on, but the bigger picture is this: I'm not saying we should eat more fried *fast* food. We should be eating more fried *good* food. I would venture to say that it just might enhance your quality of life.

CHICKEN CUTLETS

Serves 2 to 4

Chicken breasts sliced thin and pounded flat (scaloppine) are most often used to make chicken cutlets. That's okay if you have a whole chicken that you are planning on breaking down and using in other recipes. After all, you have to use the breasts for something.

If you do not have a whole chicken and are instead planning on visiting the butcher to buy chicken breasts so you can make chicken cutlets: Don't. Buy chicken thighs instead. They are way more flavorful and don't dry out in the same way. Get your butcher to bone out the thighs for you or do it yourself. It's not difficult when you have a sharp knife.

Serve these with a nice salad.

Instructions

Place a chicken thigh between two pieces of plastic wrap. Use a meat tenderizer or a rolling pin to pound the chicken flat until it is considerably wider and less than ¼ inch thick. Be careful not to tear the chicken. Repeat with the remaining thighs. Season the flattened pieces with salt all over.

Meanwhile, fill a wide skillet with ½ inch of the oil, to a temperature of 340°–350°F.

Spread the flour on one dinner plate and the bread crumbs on another. Use enough for all of the chicken, which will probably be less than you think. Beat the egg(s) with a pinch of salt and a splash of water in a bowl wide enough to accommodate a flattened thigh.

Dip each thigh in the flour, then egg, then coat with the bread crumbs on both sides, shaking off any excess each time.

Fry a couple of pieces at a time until nicely browned on both sides and cooked through to 165°F, turning over once. Drain on a wire rack over paper towels and serve with the wedges of lemon.

INGREDIENTS

4 boneless, skinless chicken thighs

Salt

Olive oil for frying

Flour for dredging

Incredibly finely ground Basic Bread Crumbs (page 124)

1–2 eggs (if your chicken thighs are on the larger side, use 2)

Lemon wedges for serving

BREADED FRIED EGGPLANT

Serves 2

Choose firm, supple eggplant with taut, unblemished skin.
Eggplant that is starting to soften and whose skin feels
looser has probably been sitting around a while and won't
be nearly as rewarding to cook and eat.

Many recipes call for salting and rinsing eggplant ahead
of time to leach out any bitterness. I find that buying
better eggplant pretty much solves that problem, but I
leave it up to you. When I do decide to first salt eggplant, I
sometimes make a brine with salt, cold water, and the juice
of a lemon and submerge the eggplant for about half an
hour. Drain and dry on clean kitchen towels before using.

Instructions

Cover a dinner plate in flour, and another with the bread
crumbs. Use just enough for all of the eggplant pieces,
which will probably be less than you think. Beat the egg
with a small pinch of salt in a third bowl.

Trim the eggplant, then cut lengthwise into ¼-inch-thick
slices. Pat them dry on both sides.

Fill a wide skillet with about ½ inch of olive oil and heat
to 340°F. Dip each eggplant slice in the flour, then egg,
then coat completely with the bread crumbs on both sides,
shaking off any excess each time. Fry a few eggplant slices
at a time until crisp and golden brown, 2 to 3 minutes.

Drain on paper towels, or on a wire rack set over paper
towels to keep them crisp, and lightly salt. Eat as is, or with
a squeeze of lemon, if desired.

INGREDIENTS

Flour

Finely ground Basic Bread
Crumbs (page 124)

1 egg

Salt

1 medium eggplant

Olive oil for frying

Lemon wedges for serving (optional)

PIZZA DI PATATE,
OR POTATO CAKE

Serves 2 to 4

This is not a pizza, or at least what most people think of as pizza. It's more like a savory stuffed potato cake, and it works best as a light meal with a salad.

INGREDIENTS

5 medium russet potatoes, or another low-moisture variety, peeled (about 2⅓ pounds/1.06 kilograms)

Salt

3 medium red onions

Olive oil

A small spoonful of tomato paste (strattu)

2–3 canned tomatoes or 6–8 fresh cherry tomatoes

Freshly ground black pepper

5 whole salted anchovies

8–9 oil-cured black olives

2 eggs

One 3.5-ounce (100-gram) chunk aged Pecorino, grated (about 1¼ cups)

1 cup (100 grams) Basic Bread Crumbs (page 124)

Instructions

Place the potatoes in a large pot and cover with water by a few inches. Bring to a boil, add a few generous pinches of salt, and cook until tender.

Meanwhile, cut the onions into ⅛- to ¼-inch slices—not too thin, because you want them to retain some texture after cooking. Add them to a wide skillet or sauté pan with a generous amount of olive oil, salt lightly, and cook over medium-low heat until soft and sweet but without browning the onions at all.

Dissolve the tomato paste in a little warm water, then add to the pan. Crush the tomatoes by hand or cut them in half, depending on their size, and add them as well. You don't want tomato sauce here; you want cooked onions with a little tomato. Season with a little more salt and cook until the tomatoes have broken down and the mixture is thick and soft. Remove from the heat, check for salt, and season with the pepper.

Rinse the anchovies and rub off their salt. Discard the fins, then the spines, creating a total of 10 fillets. Pit the olives.

Preheat the oven to 400°F.

Once the potatoes are cooked, remove them from the water, and while they are still warm, pass them through a potato ricer into a bowl. Beat the eggs and add them to the riced potatoes along with the grated cheese and a small handful of bread crumbs. Mix well, taste for salt and →

add, as needed. If the potato mixture is too wet or soft to hold shape when you take some in your hand and make a small patty, add a dusting of flour a little at a time until it comes together. You should be able to avoid this, but if you can, use as little as possible.

Liberally grease a straight-sided 8-inch cake pan with olive oil. Press half the potato mixture into an even layer in the bottom of the pan, using wet hands to smooth out the surface and seal any cracks or fissures. Cover the potatoes in the pan with the cooked onion-tomato mixture, then layer with the anchovy fillets and the olives, distributing them relatively evenly over the surface to ensure some anchovy and olive in every piece.

Shape the remaining half of the potato mixture into several large patties, and use those to make the next layer in the pan; the patties should touch each other and cover the anchovy-olive layer completely. Smooth the surface with wet hands. Finally scatter an even layer of the bread crumbs on top and drizzle with more olive oil. Bake until the bread crumbs take on color, 20 to 25 minutes.

Cool on a wire rack, trivet, or towel for about 10 minutes. Run a paring knife along the inside edge of the potato cake to dislodge it from the pan.

Hold a large plate over the top of the pan and quickly invert. The potato cake should release easily. Remove the pan, place another plate on the exposed bottom of the potato cake, and invert the entire assemblage so the top of the cake is in its rightful place.

Remove the top plate. All of this needs to happen quickly and gently. You might be familiar with this set of gestures if you make frittata or Spanish tortilla often. Allow to cool until just warmer than room temperature before slicing into wedges and serving.

POTATO CROQUETTES

Serves 2 to 4 (makes about 12)

If a mozzarella stick and a tater tot had a baby, it would be a potato croquette. If you love potatoes, you should make this snack.

INGREDIENTS

2 large russet potatoes (500–600 grams) or another extra-starchy, low-moisture potato, peeled and cut into large chunks

Salt

3.5 ounces (95 grams) Pecorino Romano and Parmigiano Reggiano cheeses, grated together (about 1 cup total)

2 eggs, separated into yolks and whites

2 ounces (60 grams) dry/low-moisture mozzarella (such as Caputo Brothers Creamery's fior di pizza), cut into 12–13 short strips

Flour

1½ cups (150 grams) finely ground Basic Bread Crumbs (page 124)

Olive, peanut, or refined sunflower oil for frying

Freshly ground black pepper

Instructions

Place the potatoes in a pot and cover with cold water. Bring to a boil and salt generously. Cook until the potatoes are quite tender (really soft). Remove with a slotted spoon, and, while they are still hot, pass them through a potato ricer into a wide shallow bowl to cool slightly.

Mix in the grated cheeses. Add salt gradually, tasting as you go, while mixing. Stir in one of the egg yolks; you may not need all of the other one, depending on the moisture level of the potatoes and the size of the eggs. The mixture should not be too wet, and should be able to hold a shape.

Form a small handful of the potato mixture into a palm-size patty. Lay a strip of the mozzarella down the center and enclose the potato around it completely. Use both hands to create a smooth exterior, shaping the patty into an oblong croquette. Repeat to form 12 or 13 pieces total.

Place the flour and bread crumbs in separate bowls. Use a fork to whisk the egg whites in a shallow bowl until they are a little frothy. Roll each croquette through flour, then the beaten egg whites, then the bread crumbs, and set on a small tray or a baking sheet in the refrigerator to rest for a few hours.

When you are ready to fry, fill a wide skillet with at least ½ inch of olive oil and heat to 340°F. Working in batches of three or four, gently add the croquettes to the hot oil; cook until nicely and evenly browned, about 3 minutes, turning them as needed. Use a slotted spoon to transfer them to paper towels, or a wire rack set atop paper towels to keep them crisp, to cool. Eat them while they're still warm. Add pepper to taste.

FRIED LAMB CHOPS

Serves 2

This method results in lamb that is medium to well done. Normally, I would quit speaking to someone if they served beautiful lamb chops cooked past medium-rare. But here, the greater degree of doneness works well. If you prefer the lamb to be pinker in the center, don't pound the chops as flat, and fry in hotter oil.

These are straightforward and lovely served with a bright salad or cooked greens.

Instructions

Use a meat tenderizer, pestle, or rolling pin to slightly flatten the lamb chops, being careful not to detach the meat from the bone. Rub the lamb chops on both sides with salt and allow to sit on a plate at room temperature, about 10 minutes.

Beat the egg in a shallow dish. Prepare a dish of flour and a dish of the bread crumbs. Dip each lamb chop in the flour, then the egg, then coat well with the bread crumbs, shaking off any excess each time. (Discard any leftover coating ingredients.)

Heat about ½ inch of olive oil in a wide skillet with high sides (to avoid splatters), over medium heat. Once the oil shimmers, add the coated lamb chops. Fry, flipping once, until browned and crisp, about 2 minutes for the first side and a minute for the second (you want an interior temperature of 130°–140°F). Drain on paper towels for a moment before serving.

INGREDIENTS

4 bone-in lamb rib chops

Salt

1 egg

Flour for dredging

⅓–½ cup (30–50 grams) medium to finely ground Basic Bread Crumbs (page 124)

Olive oil or other preferred oil for frying

154

Rice balls:
arancini vs. suppli

Both covered with bread crumbs, suppli and arancini are generally referred to as rice balls in the United States, but don't be confused. They are different.

For starters, arancini, meaning "little oranges," are definitively Sicilian. In Palermo and the western part of the island, they are round and about the size of a small orange, although sometimes a little larger, but not typically the softball size found in some old-school Brooklyn establishments. In Catania and the east, they are conical, generally smaller, and do not resemble an orange, but they do share the same name. There is also a division between eastern and western Sicily as to whether or not the noun is masculine or feminine, but I will leave it to the Sicilians to parse that one for themselves.

Arancini date back to the tenth century, when the island was under Arab rule. Their insides commonly contain rice that is boiled, peas, a meat ragu, maybe a little tomato (not a tenth-century ingredient), and saffron, although you may encounter a fake version of that deeply colored spice in the arancini sold as street food. Sicilians and people elsewhere now make all manner of arancini, but the classic ones are stuffed with ragu and peas; the cheese used in those should only be caciocavallo.

Suppli are said to have been invented in nineteenth-century Rome. Snack-size and oblong or oval in shape, they are made with rice that is often cooked in the fashion of a risotto rather than boiled. Tomato sauce and mozzarella are classic ingredients, with sausage, ground meat, and/or chicken organs added in plentiful and more modern times. The version presented here (page 162) is vegetarian and a little more stripped down.

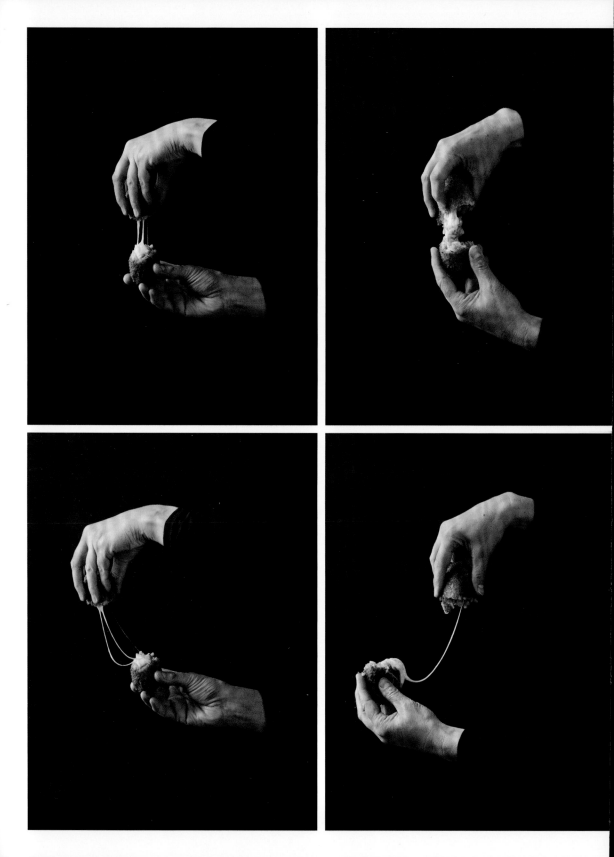

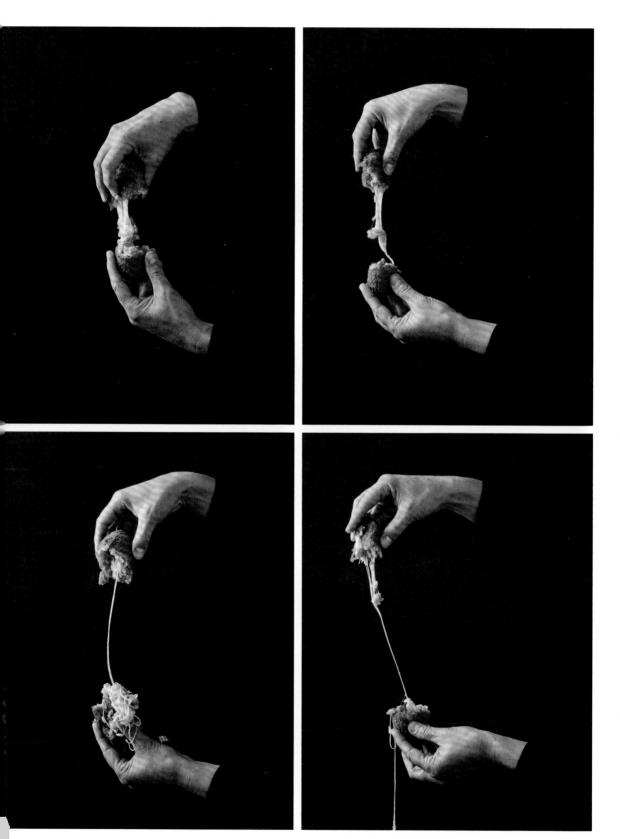

ARANCINI

Makes 16 to 20

You can make rice in advance as well as stuff and shape the arancini and refrigerate before frying.

Instructions

For the rice: Combine 4½ cups water, the salt, and the rice in a medium pot. Bring to a boil, then cook, uncovered, until the rice has absorbed all of the water and is tender, stirring as needed to keep it from sticking. Crumble the saffron threads into a small bowl and cover with a little warm water to bloom for 10 minutes while the rice is cooking. Once the rice is done, remove it from the heat and stir in the butter or lard and the saffron with its soaking water. Spread the finished rice on a small baking sheet lined with lightly greased parchment paper and place it in the refrigerator for an hour or two to cool and firm up while you make the ragu (or filling, if that's how you want to look at it).

For the ragu: Finely chop the onion, carrot, and celery and place in a sauté pan. Add a good drizzle of olive oil, stir to coat, and cook slowly over medium-low heat. Once the vegetables are soft but not browned, toss in the bay leaf and the cinnamon stick. Add the meat in pinches, and cook, stirring, until it loses its raw look. Increase the heat and deglaze the pan with a splash of the white wine. Cook it off for a few minutes (to reduce the wine's alcohol). Thin a spoonful of the tomato paste and stir it into the meat. Add enough water to barely cover the mixture, season lightly with salt, reduce the heat, and cook slowly, uncovered, for at least 1 hour, adding the peas toward the end of cooking. Discard the bay leaf and cinnamon stick, and grate in some of the aged cheese. Season with pepper. Taste, and adjust the salt as needed. Allow to cool before making the arancini.

INGREDIENTS

For the rice

Salt

2 cups (400 grams) raw arborio or carnaroli rice

Pinch of saffron threads

2 tablespoons (25–30 grams) unsalted butter or lard

For the ragu

Half an onion

1 small carrot

1 small celery rib

Olive oil

1 bay leaf

One 3-inch cinnamon stick

1 cup (200 grams) ground meat (all beef, or beef and pork)

Splash of dry white wine

Concentrated tomato paste, preferably strattu (see Resources, page 225)

Salt

Handful frozen peas

1.5–2 ounces (40–50 grams) of caciocavallo cheese (or substitute Parmigiano Reggiano)

Freshly ground black pepper

For assembly

Flour

Sparkling water

Finely ground Basic Bread
Crumbs (see page 124)

Olive, peanut, or refined
sunflower oil for frying

For assembly: When you are ready to make the arancini, make a loose batter with about ¾ cup flour and 1½ cups sparkling water (slightly thicker than a pancake batter) and place your bread crumbs on a plate or tray. Heat about 3 inches of oil in a deep pot to about 330°F. Line a tray with paper towels and set a wire rack over it.

Using damp hands, take a handful of the cooled rice—the size of a small orange, about 2½ inches across—and shape it into a concave disk. Fill the center with a few spoonfuls of the ragu mixture. Encase it inside the disk and seal, to make a smooth, compact ball. Once you have finished with all of the rice and filling, pass each one through the batter and then roll in the bread crumbs to completely cover. (You may have filling left over, which can be refrigerated for up to 3 days.)

Deep-fry just a few at a time in the hot oil until they are nicely browned and the interior is heated through. Drain on the wire rack.

SUPPLI

Makes 12 to 20

This is street food, something you'd eat before your pizza. They are popular in Rome, and if we made them in the U.S., they'd be popular here, too.

Instructions

Bring the broth to a boil in a saucepan, then reduce the heat to a simmer.

Pour a thin coat of the oil into a wide skillet. Stir in the onions and cook over medium heat until they are slightly softened. Add the rice, stir well, and toast for a few minutes, stirring to prevent sticking.

Add a small ladle of the simmering broth to the skillet to just barely cover the rice. Pour in the tomato passata and stir well. Cook over medium heat, stirring almost constantly to release the starch in the rice. As the liquid evaporates and the tomato-rice mixture thickens and begins to stick to the bottom of the pan, add more broth— just a little at a time—to keep the mixture loose and somewhat fluid until the rice is cooked, but still al dente with a little starchiness at the core. It will continue to cook a little off the heat, and further when you fry the suppli. You want the finished rice mixture a little tighter and drier than a risotto. (You may not use all the broth.)

Once you have achieved the right consistency, turn off the heat, stir in the grated cheese, and season with salt and pepper. Spread the finished rice on a small baking sheet lined with lightly greased parchment paper and place it in the refrigerator for an hour or two to cool and firm up.

Whisk the eggs in a bowl and season with a little salt. Place the bread crumbs in a separate bowl. Grab enough rice to fill the palm of your hand. If it holds its shape when you compress it, press the rice into a thickish, concave disk and dot the center of the disk with cubes of the mozzarella.

INGREDIENTS

4 cups (950 ml) vegetable broth (you can substitute lightly salted water)

Olive oil

1 small onion, finely chopped

2 cups (400 grams) raw arborio or carnaroli rice

1¾ cups (400 grams) tomato passata (puree) or whole canned tomatoes passed through a food mill

Slightly less than ½ cup (about 40 grams) grated Pecorino Romano or Parmigiano Reggiano

Salt

Freshly ground black pepper

2–3 eggs

2 cups (200 grams) finely ground Basic Bread Crumbs (page 124)

5½-7 ounces (150–200 grams) dry/low-moisture mozzarella (such as Caputo Brothers Creamery's fior di pizza), cut into small cubes or thin strips

Olive, peanut, or refined sunflower oil for frying

Enclose the cheese inside, sealing the rice into an oval or cylinder. Make some effort to keep the thickness of the rice somewhat consistent and smooth out any cracks or openings with damp hands. You want to make sure the mozzarella is fully covered.

Repeat to use all of the rice and mozzarella, wetting your hands as needed for easy shaping. You should be able to make many good-size suppli. Roll each one through the beaten eggs and then coat completely with the bread crumbs. You can repeat this process for an extra-thick crust and somewhat crisper outsides, if desired. Place the breaded suppli on a tray or a plate and refrigerate, uncovered, while you heat the oil to fry them.

Heat 2-3 inches of oil in a deep saucepan, to about 330°F. You want to fry the suppli, in small batches to a golden brown, a little cooler than you fry some other items so they can heat through and melt the mozzarella inside without getting too dark on the outside. Line a tray with paper towels and set a wire rack over it. Drain on the wire rack and let them rest for only a minute or two—you'll want to eat the suppli while they are still hot, for the full melted cheese experience.

It would be remiss of me to write a book on how to eat bread that only included things to make with bread, because the pairing of a dish with a hunk of bread is essential eating for many cultures around the world.

I eat bread with every meal, whether it's in the dish itself or on the side. I've had many a night with a red cabbage salad and a grapefruit salad and a slice of bread as a light meal. And as for the Led Zeppelin Salad (page 173)—I can have just about anything on the table, but when that tremendous dish comes out it's the best thing there by a long shot.

While I do eat and cook meat, I don't really do it that much at home. I like to cook and eat really nice beans and vegetables, and they're better for you. Vegetables at peak, cultivated with care, from farmers who aspire to make really nice food, brings me great joy and, I hope, you too.

RED CABBAGE SALAD

Serves 2 to 4

Cabbage gets a bad rap. But this salad is lovely all year round, especially when the cabbage is cut super-thin with care, studded with the finest capers you can find, dressed with fresh herbs, and well seasoned. Serve with a hunk of bread for lunch.

Instructions

Use an extremely sharp knife to cut the cabbage as finely as possible into lengths long enough that you are not making relish and short enough that they aren't awkward to eat (2 to 3 inches). Soak the cut cabbage in a large bowl of ice water for 10 to 15 minutes; this will help the cabbage stay crisp in the salad.

Rinse the capers, rubbing off their salt, then soak them in a small bowl of cold water while preparing the other ingredients. Mince the garlic or smash it to a fine paste with a pinch of salt in a mortar and pestle. Finely chop the parsley and pick the mint leaves from their stems.

Drain the cut cabbage and dry it in a salad spinner, or place it in a clean dry pillowcase and swing it around fast (doing this outside is best). Transfer it to a large bowl.

Drain the capers and add them to the cabbage, along with the garlic, parsley, and mint leaves. Season well with salt and pepper. Dress with a light squeeze of lemon juice, the vinegar, and a dash of olive oil—but not too much that the leaves are heavy or laden with it.

INGREDIENTS

1 small, tight head of red cabbage about 4 inches in diameter, or half of a larger head (slightly less than 2 pounds/about 800 grams)

2 tablespoons (30 grams) salted capers (or substitute oil-cured black olives, pitted)

1 small garlic clove

½ bunch fresh flat-leaf parsley

Leaves from a few sprigs of mint

Salt

Freshly ground black pepper

Half a lemon

A drop or two of red wine vinegar

Olive oil

EGGPLANT SALAD

Serves 1 or 2

Boiling eggplant may seem strange. Most people eat the vegetable fried, roasted, grilled, or cooked in some other fashion that allows the eggplant to absorb the flavor from its cooking method or the other ingredients in the dish. Boiling eggplant is unapologetic, and lets the flavor of the vegetable stand on its own, heightened only with a simple dressing. Use bread as a utensil for eating this salad.

INGREDIENTS

Salt

1 small to medium Italian eggplant

1 small garlic clove

1 small red dried chile pepper

Red wine vinegar

Olive oil

A few fresh mint leaves or fresh oregano leaves

Instructions

Bring a large pot of water to a rolling boil, and salt it generously. Carefully drop the whole eggplant into the pot; it will float. Boil the eggplant, turning it often to make sure it cooks relatively evenly, until the interior feels completely soft when pierced with a fork or a thin skewer, 15 to 25 minutes.

Peel the eggplant while it's still warm. Discard pockets of seeds if you like. Cut the flesh from top to bottom into thin strips and place in a bowl.

Mince the garlic and add it to the eggplant. Finely slice some of the chile pepper (to taste) and add it to the bowl. Season the mixture with salt, then dress with a few drops of the vinegar and a generous pour of olive oil. Add a few whole (or torn if large) mint or oregano leaves and mix well.

Either serve immediately or allow the dish to sit for a while at room temperature so the flavors can mature.

INSALATA COTTO E CRUDO, OR LED ZEPPELIN SALAD

Serves 2

INGREDIENTS

2 medium (320 grams) red onions

Olive oil

Salt

4 small to medium waxy red potatoes (680–850 grams total)

1 cup (250 grams) fresh green beans

1 pint (275 grams) cherry tomatoes

12 oil-cured black olives, pitted

1 garlic clove

Small escarole hearts or romaine hearts, to your liking (optional)

1 cup (164 grams) cooked chickpeas (optional)

Freshly ground black pepper

Dried Italian oregano

Red wine vinegar

Juice of half a lemon

1–2 hard to semi-soft cooked eggs, depending on your preference

Canned tuna, preferably in oil (optional)

In Palermo, vegetable vendors are seemingly on every corner. In addition to the beautiful displays of fresh produce, most sell boiled potatoes, boiled green beans, roasted onions and peppers, cooked chickpeas, and dressed olives. This is incredibly convenient. It gets very hot in the summer, and, as I learned on a trip to Sicily, kitchens in some Palermo apartments can be small—as in, two burners and no oven small. Serve this with Pizza Bianca (page 25) or focaccia—or buy some special bread for eating with what will become a favorite salad.

Those cooked items from the market combined with some choice raw vegetables make the greatest of all summer salads—so great that an old friend referred to it as Led Zeppelin salad. Because most of us don't have the good fortune to live in Sicily, we have to cook these vegetables ourselves. American kitchens are larger and you probably have air conditioning or at least four burners and an oven, so it's not that hard even in the dead of summer. This is one of my all-time favorite meals with bread because it is a celebration of peak summer produce.

Instructions

Preheat the oven to 400°F.

Slice the red onions ¼ to ½ inch thick, laying them on a baking sheet as you work. Drizzle with olive oil and lightly salt. Roast, turning once after they just begin to brown.

Alternatively, lightly oil and salt the onions, then wrap together in foil. Place the foil package on a baking sheet and roast until completely soft, 35 to 45 minutes. This method takes longer, but provides a slightly different but pleasing texture and flavor. Unwrap, cool, and separate into largish pieces. →

Meanwhile, scrub the potatoes and place in a large pot. Cover with cold water, add a generous pinch of salt, and place over medium-high heat. Fill a large bowl with water and ice cubes.

While the water with the potatoes is coming up to a boil, trim the tops of your green beans and de-string, as needed. Once the potatoes are nearly cooked, toss in the green beans and cook until they are soft. You don't want them to turn to mush, but you are also not looking for blanched and shocked green beans. Use tongs to transfer them to the ice water bath to cool down.

Once the potatoes are cooked, use a slotted spoon to transfer them to a clean dish towel; discard their skins while they are still warm. Quarter or halve the potatoes (depending on their size) and place in a large mixing bowl. Drain and dry the green beans and add them to the potatoes. Add the cooked onions.

Cut each cherry tomato in half and add to the bowl. Pit the olives and mince the garlic; add both to the bowl. Rinse and dry the escarole or romaine hearts, if using, then cut or pull them into small pieces and add to the bowl. Drain the chickpeas, if using, and add. Season everything with salt, pepper, and dried oregano. Dress with a few drops of vinegar and some lemon juice, and a generous amount of olive oil. Serve each portion garnished with an egg, and tuna if you'd like.

GRAPEFRUIT SALAD

Serves 2

This salad is great in winter when citrus is at its peak and most produce becomes hard to find and you need something to keep yourself from total despair. Use the bread of your choice to sop up the olive oil and citrus bits as you finish the dish.

INGREDIENTS

2 large grapefruit (the red ones are nice, but this recipe will work with any variety)

Olive oil

Salt

Freshly ground (coarse) black pepper or dried chile pepper flakes

Instructions

Peel and cut the grapefruit into supremes. If you know how to do this, skip the next three paragraphs. If not:

Peel the grapefruit by cutting off the tops and bottoms. Set flat on a cutting board, and cut away the peel and pith with a knife, following the contours of the fruit and without removing any flesh. Cut off any bits of white pith that may remain. With practice and a sharp knife, you should be able to have a perfectly round, peeled grapefruit with a slightly flat top and bottom and no traces of pith.

Hold the grapefruit in your nondominant hand over a bowl to collect any juices, then cut supremes from the grapefruit by slicing between the membranes. You should be able to get relatively even half-moon segments of fruit with no membrane. Divide your mostly dry grapefruit supremes between two plates.

Squeeze the fleshy grapefruit (membrane) mass in your hand into a small bowl to extract all the juice that's left. Drink the juice, or save it for another use.

Dress the grapefruit supremes with olive oil. Season with salt and either black pepper or chile flakes.

CELERY SALAD

Serves 2

I first had a celery salad at the restaurant Etto in Washington, D.C., owned by Peter Pastan and the late Tad Curtz. Whimsically called "celery celery celery" on the menu, it featured celery stalks, celery hearts, and celery leaves. As I recall, it also featured walnuts and some shaved Pecorino. Here's my own take.

Look for celery that is green and crisp and still has its leaves. If your celery is sad and wilted, soak it in a bowl of ice water briefly to help restore its crunch. You can remove the strings from the celery if it is excessively stringy, but if not, you are cutting it finely enough that it shouldn't matter much when you are eating it. Serve with bread, and maybe a piece of young sheep's-milk cheese on the side.

INGREDIENTS

A few salted capers

1 whole stalk (bunch) celery, plus a few of its leaves

1 small garlic clove

A handful fresh mint leaves

Pinch of salt

Lemon quarter or half

Olive oil

Freshly ground black pepper

Instructions

Rinse the capers to remove the salt, then soak them in a small bowl of cold water for about 10 minutes.

Cut each celery rib into thin half-moons and place in a bowl. Cut the garlic into very thin slices and add them to the bowl. If your celery leaves and mint leaves are small and delicate, add them to the salad whole; otherwise, chiffonade (roll up and finely slice) before tossing in the bowl.

Drain the capers (discarding the liquid) and add them as well. Salt the salad and lightly toss. Dress with a squeeze of lemon juice, a drizzle of olive oil, and some pepper. Toss again before serving.

PUNTARELLE

Serves 2

Puntarelle is among my favorites of all vegetables. It is a salad staple in Rome all winter, but available for a shorter window here in the northeastern United States. This is one of a handful of salad recipes that go nicely with a loaf of bread. As a matter of fact, you can make a series of salads to go with your bread and you'll be set for a meal that looks modest but is actually rather decadent. Now, back to the puntarelle. I am fortunate to have access to the produce grown by Jessi Okamoto and Chris Field at Campo Rosso Farm in eastern Pennsylvania. They are well known in the New York City area and beyond for their production of specialty chicories, and their puntarelle is of a remarkable quality (as is pretty much everything else they grow).

Puntarelle is also known as asparagus chicory, because the shoots with their tips visually resemble asparagus. They are much crisper and lighter than asparagus, however, and have a pleasing, refreshing bitterness.

To prepare a salad with puntarelle, it is worth investing in a taglià puntarelle, or puntarelle cutter. A quick internet search will give you some options for purchase. You can also cut the puntarelle shoots with a knife, but that is a lot more work.

Instructions

Separate the leaves from the heads of the puntarelle and reserve for another use; they are perfect for Fava Bean Puree with Bitter Greens (page 203) or just for some sautéed chicory. Take the tender shoots and cut off the bottoms toward the root if they are fibrous or woody. Pass them through your puntarelle cutter (or slice into thin strips) and into a bowl of ice water. Let them hang out there until they curl up. →

Meanwhile, make a dressing with 1 small garlic clove, 1 or 2 salted and rinsed anchovy fillets, a squeeze of lemon juice, and a drizzle of olive oil. This is a great use for a mortar and pestle or, if you are so inclined, an immersion (stick) blender or other tool that will allow you to emulsify the mixture.

Remove the now-curled puntarelle strips from their ice bath and shake dry. Toss in a bowl with the dressing and a little salt. A touch of black pepper can be nice. Top with more salted and rinsed anchovy fillets before serving.

PURSLANE SALAD

Serves 2

INGREDIENTS

1 large bunch purslane
(1 pound/454 grams)

1 small red onion

A dash of red wine vinegar (optional),
plus a few drops for dressing the salad

1 smallish cucumber

½ pint (10–12) sweet cherry tomatoes

A few sprigs fresh mint

A few sprigs fresh flat-leaf parsley

Salt

1 lemon

Olive oil

Freshly ground black pepper

Purslane is eaten all over the world. In France it is called *pourpier*, in Italy *porcellana*, in Spanish it is known as *verdolaga*, in Turkey they call it *semizotu*, and in Arabic it is called الرجلة. It is eaten in all manner of soups, salads, and stews, and in almost every fashion imaginable. But in America, it is largely considered a weed. You probably have it in your backyard or your garden or have seen it growing through the cracks in the sidewalk. It is almost literally everywhere.

In addition to having great flavor and texture, purslane is ideal for salads in the summer when it is too hot for most lettuces or other more delicate greens. It is also insanely good for you, with a higher amount of omega-3 fatty acids than any other plant (if you are into that sort of thing). Pair it with a slab of Pizza Bianca (page 25) or a hunk of crusty bread for a light summer meal.

Instructions

Clean the purslane by soaking it in a bowl of cold water. You might need to lift it out and rinse it a few times, depending on how dirty it is. Pick the paddle-shaped leaves off the thick central stems, leaving the small clusters of leaves intact and including the more tender smaller shoots of the main stem. The stems contain most of the plant's oxalic acid, which gives a pleasant, slightly sour taste; that taste is more noticeable when the purslane is picked early in the morning. Once you are finished cleaning, dry the leaves and leaf clusters on kitchen towels, in a salad spinner, or with the old pillowcase trick (insert, close, swing in quick rotations). Place the dry leaves in a large bowl.

Cut the onion in half from top to bottom (through the root end), trim off the ends, and cut each half vertically into thin slices. Taste one; if the onion's bite is too sharp, →

soak the slices in a bowl of ice-cold water with a dash of vinegar for about 10 minutes. Drain, breaking up the slices into thin strips, and add to the purslane.

If the cucumber's skin is tough, peel the cucumber or partially peel it by using a vegetable peeler to create alternating lengthwise stripes. Cut the cucumber in half lengthwise, and scoop out the seeds with the tip of a spoon. Cut the halves crosswise into half-moons about ⅛ inch thick. Add them to the purslane.

Halve the cherry tomatoes and toss in the bowl, along with the mint and parsley leaves picked from their sprigs. If the leaves are small, feel free to leave them whole. You can also chiffonade (roll up and finely slice) them.

Salt the salad and toss. Add a few drops of red wine vinegar, squeeze in the juice of the lemon, add a drizzle of olive oil, and throw in some pepper. Toss again to coat evenly, and serve.

WINTER SQUASH WITH HOT PEPPER, GARLIC, AND MINT

Serves 2 to 4

Don't underestimate the deliciousness of this dish. It makes a good topping for grilled or toasted bread, a filling for a sandwich, or a side dish.

INGREDIENTS

2 pounds (about 900 grams) densely fleshed winter squash or pumpkin, such as kabocha, kuri, or even butternut

Olive oil

Salt

1 garlic clove

1 fresh hot red chile pepper (or substitute sliced hot peppers preserved in oil), seeds and stem discarded

White wine vinegar

A handful fresh mint leaves

Instructions

Prepare a grill for direct heat.

Use a sharp knife or sturdy vegetable peeler to peel the squash. Cut it in half and remove the seeds (save, clean, and roast them if you choose, or discard). Cut into wedges no more than 1 inch thick, or into slices thick enough to grill. Toss in a bowl with just enough olive oil and salt to coat evenly. Grill over a hot fire until softened and maybe even blackened in spots, turning as needed. Transfer to a wide, shallow bowl.

Thinly slice the garlic and the fresh hot pepper; add both to the bowl. Season with salt, then add a few drops of the vinegar and the mint. Dress with more olive oil and toss gently to coat. Let this marinate at room temperature for at least 2 hours before serving.

Alternatively, you can fry the cut-up squash until tender in olive oil or your preferred frying oil, drain on a wire rack, and dress in the same fashion.

SAUTÉED PEPPERS WITH OLIVES

Serves 2

I first encountered this remarkably simple dish in Naples, served at a bakery in a neighborhood high on a hillside overlooking the Gulf of Naples. On the counter they had enormous three-kilo pagnotte, an oblong loaf, and also sold a variety of room-temperature vegetable dishes and a few fried things. In fact, there are a number of bakeries in Naples like this, which is one reason why Naples is one of my favorite cities on Earth.

I bought a quarter kilo of bread and a few hundred grams of Carmen peppers, and we made rough sandwiches that we ate on the sidewalk before continuing our walk.

Note: If you can't find Gaeta olives, look for Turkish "midway" olives, or Greek Kalamata, or even Alphonso. None of those are quite right, but they will work.

Instructions

Cut the onion from top to bottom, trim off the ends, and cut each half vertically into slices between ⅛ and ¼ inch thick.

Trim off the tops of the peppers, take out the seeds and ribs, cut in half lengthwise, and cut into strips on the diagonal, 1–1½ inches wide.

Drizzle some olive oil in a skillet, add the onions, and start the heat on medium-low. Once the onions begin cooking, add the peppers and a pinch of salt, and stir. When the peppers are mostly cooked, toss in the olives and continue cooking until the peppers' skins begin to wrinkle, about 30 minutes. Deglaze the pan with a tablespoon or two of the vinegar and remove from the heat. Mix in the parsley leaves and serve at room temperature.

INGREDIENTS

1 smallish red onion

4–5 medium elongated sweet peppers (substitute a mix of red and yellow bell peppers, if you must)

Olive oil

Salt

12–15 cured Gaeta olives, pitted (see headnote)

White wine vinegar

A few leaves fresh flat-leaf parsley

BEANS AND PEAS

Here is a combination of bread-and-bean dishes and bean dishes with which I strongly recommend you eat bread. I've even had a fantasy about opening a restaurant called Bean World, but I have not because I know it wouldn't go over well. (I did have Bean World pop-ups at Bitter Ends in Pittsburgh and at Brooks Headley's Superiority Burger in Manhattan before I had my own bakery. The events were popular enough, perhaps because it was good beans and good bread for $5.) In any event, whether it's bread in the creation of the dish or on the side as a means of soaking up the beans, mopping the plate, and giving yourself some added sustenance, bread and beans might not be pretty but they're pretty perfect together.

A few notes on beans

The first step in cooking beans is buying the right beans to cook. This is trickier than it would seem. Most of the beans found in the grocery store aren't very good. In many places, the dried beans in the bulk section don't see enough turnover to be remotely fresh.

On the packaging, there is little indication of when beans were harvested, how they've been stored (and for how long), or where they even came from in the first place. Those beans could have come from a number of different farms in a number of different conditions, even from different harvests—in which beans from two or more years ago are mixed in with last year's crop to bulk it up.

It would be easy to think, who cares? The beans are dried. It's not like they are going to go bad. While it is true that they don't become inedible per se, older beans don't cook the same way fresher ones do. You can end up with a total mess—with some of the beans completely blown away and turned into mush and some of the beans still starchy and hard. Many people avoid dried beans for this reason and instead choose canned beans. If this has happened to you, know that it was probably not your fault—you just bought crappy beans.

Don't be discouraged. Find good beans, and all will be redeemed. Look for suppliers who will guarantee that they are selling you new-crop beans, and who approach beans with the care and reverence they deserve. Rancho Gordo has excellent beans, as does Zürsun, a company out of Idaho (see Resources, page 225). More small U.S. farmers are growing a variety of beans and selling them at farmers markets. This way you can ask them directly about their beans and be assured of a good product. Such new-crop beans cost a lot more than beans in the grocery store—and they're worth it.

A cheaper alternative is to buy your beans from busy international markets that cater to bean-loving populations. This will at least give you a better chance that they are turning over their inventory and will stock a better product for people who demand it.

The next step: Soak, or don't soak? If your beans are new-crop ones that have been stored properly, you don't need to soak them. Soaking will not hurt them and does shorten the cooking time a little. Ultimately, it is your call, with the exception of chickpeas and fava beans, which you should always soak because they won't cook otherwise.

Regardless of which dried beans you have, you want to pick through or at least visually scan them to make sure there is no gravel, dirt, or foreign material. Give them a rinse, then soak them overnight in fresh cold water or place them directly in a pot and get down to business.

The choice of pot is important. My favorite way to cook beans is in clay. Glazed or unglazed terra-cotta makes a perfect cooking vessel. People have been cooking beans in clay since there were clay pots and beans. If you don't have a clay pot, use the heaviest-lidded pot you have. Enameled cast iron is a good substitute.

If you soaked your beans the night before, drain them and give them a rinse. Put them in your chosen pot and cover them with fresh water. You don't need as much as you might think: just enough to cover the beans by an inch or so will suffice. Too much water, and the flavor of the beans will be diluted and the cooking water will be less valuable later on.

You can add some aromatics at this point if you like: a clove or two of garlic or an onion, some celery, carrot, parsley, a bay leaf, maybe a few whole peppercorns, depending on what you'll be doing with the beans. I most often cook beans simply, without any aromatics, partly because I like the taste of beans, but also because it gives me more latitude in terms of where and how I use the cooked beans.

There is some argument about whether salting beans early in the process changes the way they cook. I don't salt until the end of cooking. If the beans are top-notch, I don't think it matters that much.

Place a lid on the pot and put over a burner on low heat. If you are using clay, use a heat diffuser. If you are not using clay and have a heat diffuser, use it anyway. The idea is that you want to cook the beans evenly and slowly. As they come up to a simmer, skim off any foam or froth that appears and replace the lid. Cook. Slowly. Nice and easy.

Check the beans every now and again. If your beans swell a lot in the process of cooking, absorbing a lot of water, and the pot starts to look a little dry, top off with some boiling water. When the beans are soft, salt to taste.

Store cooked beans in the refrigerator in their cooking liquid. Don't throw it away. It is useful when you want to add liquid to a bean dish and provides better flavor and texture than just using water.

Alternatively, you can cook beans in an oven in a baking dish or a hotel pan. Put the beans in the dish or pan, pour in fresh water, covering the beans by about an inch, cover tightly with foil, and set in a 200°F oven (any range of low oven temperatures will work; I just like the texture of very slowly cooked beans the best). Cook until done, checking periodically. Follow the same salting, cooling, and storage suggestions above.

A note on canned beans: Don't—really. They taste like cans. I understand that everyone is busy and says canned beans are a wonderful time-saver. Cooking dried beans isn't hard, and I maintain that slow-cooking anything actually saves you time because it is largely unattended and you can do other things in the meantime. If you must use canned beans, at least buy the ones in BPA-free paper cartons or glass jars, because they won't have a metallic taste.

PANCOTTO WITH BEANS

Serves 2 to 3

This is not a sexy dish. You probably don't want to make this soup for a date you are trying to impress or as a prelude to a night of wild lovemaking (unless your intended is incredibly special). Pancotto is beige and runs the risk of being somewhat stodgy, but it is one of the simplest, most deeply satisfying, comforting dishes you could ever make. Feel free to add escarole or a host of other vegetables, including broccoli rabe, leeks, cardoons, and asparagus, or whatever is in season.

Instructions

Heat a large skillet over medium-high heat. Add a generous drizzle of olive oil and the onion, stirring to coat.

Reduce the heat to medium-low and cook the onion slowly until soft and translucent, 6 to 10 minutes. Add the dried pepper and cook for a few minutes, until fragrant, then stir in the pieces of bread.

Add the cooked white beans and their cooking liquid. If the beans and bread are not mostly submerged, add some water and a little salt as needed (the beans and bread already contain salt).

Reduce the heat to low and simmer, stirring occasionally to break up the pieces of bread as you go, until the bread is soft. Stir more often as the beans and bread cook and thicken, adding a little more bean cooking liquid or water, as needed. The dish is finished once the bread has completely softened. Adjust the consistency with more liquid until what's in the skillet resembles a thin porridge. Taste for salt.

Serve in a shallow bowl (or bowls) with a drizzle of oil and the seeded and minced chile pepper, if desired.

INGREDIENTS

Olive oil

1 small red onion, finely chopped

1 small whole dried hot chile pepper, plus an optional seeded and minced dried hot chile pepper for serving

2 slices (200 grams) stale bread, crusts and all, torn into bite-size pieces

1½–2 cups (425 grams) cooked white beans, with their cooking liquid

Salt

DRIED PEAS WITH PUNTARELLE AND FRIED BREAD

Serves 2 to 4

INGREDIENTS

1¾ cups (250 grams) dried whole peas

1 small onion, halved

A few sprigs fresh flat-leaf parsley

Salt

A few pieces of stale bread

Olive oil, or your preferred oil for frying

2¼ pounds (1 kilo) greens from a few heads of puntarelle, or a few bunches of dandelion greens, or even a few bunches of broccoli rabe

2–3 garlic cloves

1–2 dried hot red chile peppers

Peperoni cruschi (optional; see page 102)

This is a version of an old Italian dish from the cooking of Puglia, famous for the quality of its bread. Multiple variants abound, using chickpeas or other small legumes and a variety of different bitter greens. The key here is the fried pieces of bread. Unlike different versions of pane cotto where the bread is cooked with other ingredients until it is softer and more porridge-like, frying the pieces of bread lets them stay crunchy longer in the dish and creates a nice texture as some of them begin to soften as they absorb the broth. Some cooks prefer cutting larger pieces of bread, but I like them closer to the size of the peas so you can eat them without having to wait until they completely soften.

Instructions

The day before you would like to make this, soak the dried peas overnight. The following day, place the peas in a pot with enough cold water to cover by 1–1½ inches and add the onion halves and parsley. Bring to a boil, lightly salt, and reduce to a simmer. Cook gently, covered, until tender, about 1½–2 hours. Depending on your specific peas, this might take even longer. Check for seasoning and set aside.

Meanwhile, cut the bread into cubes around ¼–½ inch. Place olive oil in a pot that will fit a handful of fried bread pieces and heat over medium heat until around 350°F. If you don't have a thermometer, test the oil temperature with a cube of bread. If it starts frying and taking color within a few seconds, you are pretty much good to go. Control your heat to prevent the oil from smoking. Fry the small bread cubes in batches until golden brown and →

crispy, then remove from the oil with a slotted spoon or spider and drain on paper towels. Reserve the oil.

Fill a large bowl with water and ice cubes. Bring a large pot of water to a boil. Generously salt your water, let it return to the boil, and, working in batches (depending on the size of your pot), boil your greens for a few minutes, remove them from the boiling water, and plunge into the bowl of ice water to cool. Remove from the ice water, squeeze dry with your hands, and coarsely chop.

Lightly crush the garlic cloves and add to a wide, shallow pot with the whole dried red peppers and some olive oil and bring up the heat to medium. When the garlic starts frying, add the cooked chopped greens, lightly salt, and stir.

Sauté the greens with the garlic and hot pepper for a few minutes before adding the cooked dried peas and enough of their cooking liquid to keep the whole thing loose. You aren't really looking for soup here, but you don't want the dish to be dry at all. Simmer for about a half hour to bring everything together, adding more pea cooking liquid if the dish begins to get dry. Check for salt.

Fry the peperoni cruschi, if using, in the same oil you used to fry the cubes of bread for a few seconds until crispy. Drain on paper towels. Lightly salt.

When you are ready to serve, place a handful of fried bread cubes in each bowl, then ladle in the greens and peas with some of their broth. Top with a few more fried bread cubes, a few peperoni cruschi or some crushed hot pepper if you prefer, and a thread of good olive oil.

GREENS AND BEANS

Serves 2 to 4

INGREDIENTS

2–3 large heads of escarole

3 cups (552 grams) cooked white beans, with their cooking liquid

Olive oil

2 garlic cloves

1 small hot dried red chile pepper, plus seeded and finely chopped chile pepper for serving

Salt

I grew up eating greens and beans (or beans and greens, depending on proportions and whom you ask). I think of it as a quintessential Pittsburgh food. It has been served in nearly every Italian restaurant in the city for as long as I can remember, and I am sure much longer. Everybody has their own take on it: you can use spinach or even kale or a mix of greens instead of escarole, and black-eyed peas or borlotti beans rather than any of the ones I list. Or serve it with a fried egg or sausage or grated cheese on top. But really, if you're not serving it with a piece of bread worthy of sopping it up, it's incomplete.

The combination of greens and beans is a natural one, and it can be found in almost all cuisines in the world that involve beans. This version is much closer to the scarola e fagioli of Campania than what I grew up on. It is humble, honest, simple food cooked in the home, and you are not likely to find it on restaurant menus outside of Pittsburgh or specific types of osterie in southern Italy. In my view, it is one of the greatest things you could ever eat. For the beans here, I suggest cannellini or controne, or dente di morto if you want to go that extra mile. (You could use Great Northerns in a pinch, but their texture would not be ideal.)

Instructions

Escarole is tricky and easily hides gritty dirt or sand in its leaves, so wash the heads well in a few changes of cold water. Cut just the greenest portion of the escarole leaves to use in this dish. The white and yellow portions brown out when cooking and are incredibly unattractive; eat those parts raw in a salad or on a sandwich. If your escarole is excessively bitter, blanch it in a large pot with vigorously boiling salted water before proceeding with the recipe. Blanched or not, cut the greens into bite-size pieces. →

Use a slotted spoon to transfer about ⅓ of the cooked beans to puree in a food processor or blender, or mash them in a mortar and pestle. Return them to their brethren in the cooking liquid and stir to thicken.

Pour a light film of olive oil into a pot large enough to hold all of the escarole and beans. Add the garlic cloves and the chile pepper, starting the heat on low. The garlic and chile pepper will slowly flavor the oil. Keep stirring and turning the cloves over after the garlic begins to sizzle and turn golden, about 6 minutes.

Add the escarole, salt to taste, and stir, increasing the heat to medium. Sauté the greens for about 10 minutes, or until they are wilted and well flavored with the garlic and pepper. Stir in the beans, their now-thickened cooking liquid, and a pinch of salt, and bring to a simmer. Cook for at least 15 minutes. If you can do this for longer over lower heat, the dish will be more flavorful. You can do it for up to an hour at a very low temperature, but the escarole will begin to turn brown after that. You want to cook it long enough that the flavors are married. Remove the whole chile and the garlic cloves. Check for salt as needed.

Serve the greens and beans in bowls with or on toasted bread with a drizzle of olive oil and a sprinkling of chopped chile pepper. I like this thick with the escarole and beans and a shallow pool of broth in the bottom of the bowl. Some people prefer it soupier.

DRIED CHESTNUT AND WHITE BEAN SOUP

Serves 2 (makes 3 to 4 cups)

INGREDIENTS

1 cup (200 grams) shelled dried chestnuts

1 cup (200 grams) dried white beans, such as cannellini

1 garlic clove

Olive oil

1 hot dried red chile pepper, plus more for serving

2 fresh or dried bay leaves

Salt

A few fresh flat-leaf parsley leaves (optional)

Ever since I was a kid, I've loved taking shopping trips to Pittsburgh's Italian markets. Meats, cheeses, olives, olive oils, vinegars, shelf upon shelf of dry pasta. As a child, I had a decent grip on what could be made with these things, but I was always drawn to the more unusual items in the stores: the crates stacked with baccalà (salt cod), barrels full of dried chestnuts, and bins with dried carob pods. I wondered what people did with them. One of the greatest pleasures of adulthood has been learning the answers to those questions. I've learned to cook a wide number of dishes that use baccalà and chestnuts. I still haven't exactly figured out the dried carob pods, which remain one of life's mysteries.

If you can't find dried chestnuts (often labeled "castagne spezzate") in your local Italian market, poke around online for a good source. You can make a slightly different version of this soup with fresh chestnuts when they are in season during the winter, but it is a lot more work to score, blanch, and peel the chestnuts before cooking (if you do, though, cook them for less time than directed below). One of the beautiful things about this dish is that with a well-stocked pantry (and yes, we should all have a supply of dry chestnuts to get through the winter) and a little forethought, all you need to buy is a loaf of bread for the table and you've got a great meal.

Instructions

Soak the chestnuts and the beans overnight in enough cold water to cover by an inch, in separate containers.

Smash the garlic with the heel of your hand or the side of a knife. Add to a heavy-bottomed pot (preferably clay, but cast iron will work) with a drizzle of olive oil and →

the whole chile pepper, and start the heat on low. Bring a saucepan of water (at least 4 cups) to a simmer on the stove.

Once the garlic begins to sizzle in the bottom of the pot, drain the beans and add them, give them a stir, and cover with some of the simmering water, by about an inch. Toss in the bay leaves. Cover and allow to cook slowly over medium-low heat.

After about an hour or so, drain the chestnuts, removing any debris that may be clinging to them. Add them to the beans in the pot, breaking them up a little more with your hands if there are large pieces. Add a little more simmering water as needed, cover, and continue to cook until the beans and chestnuts are both soft (about 1½ hours). Discard the bay leaves, the chile pepper, and the garlic (if it hasn't completely dissolved). Taste, season with salt as needed, and remove from the heat. You can puree a portion of the soup to thicken it, if desired, with a stick (immersion) blender or in a food processor.

Serve in bowls with a drizzle of olive oil and some finely chopped or coarsely ground dried chile pepper. Garnish with the parsley leaves, if desired.

FAVA BEAN PUREE WITH BITTER GREENS

Serves 6 to 8

INGREDIENTS

3¾ cups (454 grams) peeled and split dried fava beans

1 large potato (any white or yellow-fleshed variety)

Salt

Olive oil

Puntarelle or dandelion greens

1 large garlic clove

1 small dried red chile pepper

Ground red pepper for serving

Bread for serving

This is another dish in the broad category of beans and greens, though instead of being more like a soup, the beans are cooked with some potato and mashed to a satisfying puree. Most commonly associated with the cooking of Puglia, variations of this dish are found throughout southern Italy and similar dishes are common throughout the entire Mediterranean. Fava beans are one of the few Old World beans that existed in Europe and the Middle East before the discovery of the Americas. Though not listed as an ingredient, bread is an absolutely essential part of this dish. Either tear it up into small pieces and stir it into the fava puree or top the dish with small pieces of fried bread.

Instructions

Soak the fava beans overnight in enough cold water to cover by an inch.

The following day, drain the fava beans and place them in a heavy-bottomed pot—preferably a clay pot set over a heat diffuser. Peel and thinly slice the potato and add to the beans. Add enough fresh water to just cover the beans and potato, cover, and start the heat on low. Cook as slowly as possible, increasing the heat to medium-low, stirring periodically, and adding a little water as needed. It will take about 4 hours for the beans to get completely softened and for the potato to dissolve; at this point, you can mash them to a thick, smooth, homogenous puree. Season with salt and add a healthy glug of olive oil. Turn off the heat.

Bring a large pot of water to a rolling boil, and salt it generously. Add the greens and boil for a minute or two, just until softened. Drain. →

Smash the garlic clove and place it in a cold skillet with a thin film of olive oil. Start the heat on medium-low. Once the garlic begins to sizzle, add the dried chile pepper, followed by the just-drained greens. Season with salt and cook, stirring occasionally, until the greens have wilted further and are well flavored with the garlic and chile pepper. Discard the garlic and the chile pepper.

Ladle the fava bean puree into individual shallow bowls and top each with a portion of the sautéed greens. Add another healthy glug of olive oil over the greens and serve with ground red pepper at the table.

LEBLEBI

Serves 4 to 6

Leblebi is one of the most enjoyable dishes made from old bread I have ever encountered anywhere. In Tunisia, it is commonly eaten for breakfast and served almost everywhere across the country in casual restaurants.

Generally, when you order, you are given a large ceramic bowl with two spoons and a half of a stale baguette (almost always industrially produced; in this context it really works). In some cases, if leblebi is all that the establishment serves, it might already be set up on the tables.

While the cook is getting it together, you tear up the baguette into little pieces in your bowl. The server comes over and pours a ladle or two of chickpeas with all of their broth over the bread, sprinkles in a spoonful of cumin and some crushed garlic, tosses in a dollop of harissa and a generous pour of oil, and then cracks in a raw egg. This happens pretty fast. In some cases, people add a squeeze of lemon, or a few drops of vinegar, or garnish with a scattering of capers, or some pickles, and a scoop of tuna, but not always, and it certainly isn't necessary.

Once all the ingredients have been added to the bowl, you use the two spoons to mix everything together. The bread gets really soft in the chickpea liquid, and the heat of the chickpeas cooks the egg a little. The whole dish becomes like a very satisfying porridge.

About the bread: You can use other types of old bread if you like or if you don't have any baguettes around, but you might need to cook the torn pieces in the chickpea broth first depending on how stale the bread is or how hearty it was. Baguettes soften pretty fast.

You can add more baguette while you are eating if the mixture is a little thin, kind of customizing the whole thing to your taste.

Portions are generally large, but I think it is pretty easy to eat a lot of it and still feel pretty good afterward.

INGREDIENTS

2½ cups (500 grams) dried chickpeas, soaked overnight

1 red onion

A handful peeled, split fava beans (optional)

Salt

Half of a day-old baguette per serving (2–3 baguettes total), or more as needed

Ground cumin (about ¼ teaspoon per serving)

4–6 garlic cloves, crushed in a mortar and pestle with a small pinch of salt

Harissa (page 208)

Olive oil

4–6 eggs, raw, poached, or soft-boiled

Making leblebi at home, I might prefer it for lunch instead of breakfast, but either way it is pretty great.

Instructions

Drain the chickpeas and place in a large pot, with the whole onion and the fava beans, if using. Add enough water to cover them by a good 2–3 inches, lightly salt, and bring to a simmer. Cook, uncovered, until very soft. If you used the favas, they should have completely dissolved, adding a little body to the cooking liquid. Remove the onion, taste, and add salt as needed.

Alternatively, you can cook the chickpeas in the oven (see A Few Notes on Beans, page 189). Just check them periodically and make sure they remain covered with water: The whole dish depends on it.

If you're cooking chickpeas in advance—because they're likely better when they cool in their cooking liquid—reheat them before serving.

When you are ready to serve, tear up the bread into individual bowls (or cook according to the note above). Ladle the hot, cooked chickpeas with ample cooking liquid on top of the bread. For each serving, sprinkle on cumin, toss in some crushed garlic, a spoonful of harissa, a generous pour of olive oil, and an egg. Mix well, and eat while it's warm.

HARISSA

Makes 4 to 5 cups

Harissa is the most essential Tunisian condiment and a necessary part of making Leblebi (see page 206). Enjoyed in parts of Libya, Algeria, to a lesser extent Morocco, and sometimes in the couscous-consuming areas of western Sicily where the North African populations are more integrated, harissa has grown in popularity worldwide over the past few decades.

Several commercial brands are available in the United States. Sadly, most of them aren't very good and have little or nothing to do with any of the types of harissa used in Tunisia. If you don't want to make your own, at least seek out one manufactured by a small producer in Tunisia, made with minimal ingredients.

The most simple variety is a paste made only of dried, rehydrated Nabeul chiles and salt, but quite often it is seasoned with garlic and caraway and sometimes coriander or even cumin. Nabeul chiles are nearly impossible to find in the United States, so combining a few varieties of other types of dried peppers is a reasonable substitute. Nabeuls are spicy, but not crazy hot, with complex notes of raisins and stone fruit. You can play with the types of chiles and proportions of each to suit your taste while making a harissa faithful in spirit to ones found in Tunisia. I've used Italian dried peppers here because I have them readily available, but I have had great success with a combination of guajillo, New Mexico, and árbol chiles, too. It also can be nice to sneak in a morita chile or two for a touch of smokiness, but don't overdo it.

The word *harissa* comes from the Arabic term for "to pound or break into pieces," because traditionally the condiment was made in a heavy mortar and pestle. This is still a great method for small amounts, but you can use a blender or food processor for speed and convenience. It will be a little different because the blades are designed to chop, not grind, but you can get close. I've had the best luck achieving better textures using a blender, but I have also burned out more than one blender motor with

INGREDIENTS

10.6 ounces (300 grams) dried Calabrian sweet chile peppers (or substitute with a combination of guajillo, New Mexico, and árbol chiles)

1.4 ounces (40 grams) dried Calabrian hot chile peppers

3–5 garlic cloves

4½ teaspoons (10 grams) toasted caraway seeds

2 tablespoons (30 grams) salt

Olive oil

projects like this. And be prepared to stain the plastic container of your chosen device. Use caution.

Instructions

Remove the stems from the peppers and discard the seeds and ribs. Do yourself a favor and wear gloves and a mask while you do this.

Place the peppers in a bowl and cover with hot (not boiling) water and soak for 2 to 4 hours, or until they are completely soft. You may want to place a plate directly on the soaking peppers to keep them submerged. Drain thoroughly, reserving a little of the liquid.

Place the garlic (to taste) in the bowl of your blender or food processor (or mortar) with the caraway seeds and salt. Process until finely ground.

Working in batches, add the well-drained peppers, blending or pulsing until you have created a dense, thick paste. You can add a spoonful of the reserved soaking liquid if it's absolutely necessary in order to get things moving, but avoid it if you can. You want the mixture as thick as you can get it.

Pack into clean glass jars, making sure to leave no more than ¾ inch of space at the top and to eliminate any air pockets. Cover the surface with olive oil, seal the jars, and refrigerate. You can use it right away. Add oil after each time you use it, and the harissa should last about two months.

CHICKPEA SALAD

Serves 2

This salad is infinitely better if you order the beans from Rancho Gordo in Napa (see Resources, page 225). You may never eat canned beans again. It is great with a quartered boiled egg and some oil-packed tuna, if you are so inclined. Use bread as a utensil or an accompaniment.

INGREDIENTS

1½ cups (250 grams) dried chickpeas, soaked overnight, then cooked and cooled in their cooking liquid (3 cups cooked) (see A Few Notes on Beans, page 189)

1–2 ribs celery, plus a few leaves if you'd like

A few leaves fresh flat-leaf parsley

1 small red onion

Salt

Freshly ground black pepper

Red wine vinegar

Olive oil

Instructions

Drain the chickpeas from their cooking liquid and place in a bowl.

Finely chop the celery (to taste) and the parsley, and mince the red onion. Add all three ingredients to the bowl and combine with the chickpeas. Season with salt and pepper. Dress with a drop or two of the vinegar and some olive oil. Garnish with a few leaves of parsley.

I am a bread guy and not a sweets guy, which is why you won't find a laundry list of sweet things in this book. If you really need more, see French Toast (page 41) and Bread and Chocolate (page 44) in the Slices chapter. Here's the thing: I eat bread with every meal; chances are, I'm not going to also eat it for dessert. But here are some recipes, anyway. I make these for my customers and I do enjoy them on their own from time to time, as a midday something to eat with an espresso.

And as for these cereals, they're the humblest recipes in the book—the original cereal in the days before Kellogg's made Corn Flakes. They're really quite nice, especially when you're using good bread.

WARM BREAKFAST CEREAL

Serves 1

Step aside, oatmeal. This porridge is wonderful for the poor, the elderly, the infirm, the toothless, or anyone who just doesn't feel like chewing. Tear up a single piece of bread or several—as long as it's stale. Enjoy as is, or dress it up with butter, olive oil, fruits, nuts, seeds, maple syrup, honey, fresh herbs, pickles... the sky's the limit.

INGREDIENTS

Several pieces of stale rustic bread, torn (if very dry and hard, smash it into pieces however you'd like—with a rolling pin, stepped on in a baggie on the floor; be creative)

Milk (or water for a more austere version)

Salt

Instructions

Place the bread in a small pot or saucepan. Add enough milk or water to cover it almost completely. (You may need to add more as it cooks if your bread is very dry.) Season lightly with salt. Cook over medium-low heat, stirring occasionally, mashing the pieces against the side of the pot until the bread has completely softened and starts to break down, 12 to 20 minutes (max), depending on how dry the bread is and how big the pieces are.

Transfer to a warmed bowl; for a more refined texture, push the warm, softened bread mixture through a fine-mesh sieve before serving.

COLD BREAKFAST CEREAL

Instructions

Put the bread crumbs in a bowl. Pour cold milk on them. Add some sugar, if that's your thing. Eat with a spoon. Maybe it seems crazy, but is it really that different from Grape Nuts?

INGREDIENTS

Coarse bread crumbs
(lightly toasted if you wish)

Cold milk

Sugar, to taste, if desired

TORTA DI PANE

Serves 8 to 10 (makes one 10-inch cake)

This is a variation of bread pudding that is baked like a cake. With its somewhat more refined texture, it can be served in neat slices or squares instead of spoonfuls in a bowl. Traditionally, in northern Italy along the border with Switzerland, it is often spiced with cloves and/or nutmeg in addition to cinnamon. Feel free to add whatever spices you like.

INGREDIENTS

1 cup (120 grams) whole, skin-on almonds, plus a handful of blanched, peeled almonds for the top

1½–2 cups (400 grams) stale, crustless bread, in pieces

5 cups (1225 grams) whole milk

1 cup (175 grams) dried currants or raisins

Grappa or dry white wine (optional)

6 eggs

1¼ cups (250 grams) granulated sugar

Finely grated zest of 1 lemon or orange (no pith)

An incredibly small pinch of ground cinnamon

Pinch of salt

A small splash vanilla extract

8 tablespoons (113 grams) cold unsalted butter, in pieces

Confectioners' sugar for dusting

Instructions

Preheat the oven to 400°F.

Spread the cup of skin-on almonds on a small baking sheet and toast in the oven for a few minutes, until fragrant and lightly browned. Remove, leaving the oven on. Cool the almonds, then pulverize in a food processor until finely ground.

Place the stale bread pieces in a large bowl. Heat the milk in a saucepan over medium heat until bubbles form at the edges. Pour over the bread, and give the pieces enough time to rehydrate. Place the currants or raisins in a glass of grappa or white wine, if using, to plump them.

Whisk the eggs thoroughly in a separate bowl. Whisk in the granulated sugar, citrus zest, cinnamon, salt, and vanilla until well combined.

Once the bread pieces are completely soft, squeeze out and discard any excess milk. Stir in the egg mixture and your freshly ground almonds. Add the currants or raisins (if rehydrated, first drain and discard their liquid). Mix until evenly distributed.

Use some of the butter to generously grease a 10-inch springform pan and place it on a rimmed baking sheet. (Encase the bottom of your pan with foil to guard against leaks.) Pour the bread mixture into the pan, leveling →

the surface. (You may have to press it down.) Sprinkle the blanched whole almonds across the top and dot with pieces of the butter as you would like. Transfer to the oven (on the baking sheet) and immediately reduce the temperature to 375°F. Bake for 55–65 minutes (rotating the baking sheet front to back halfway through), or until the top of the cake is golden brown and a toothpick inserted into the center comes out clean.

Cool, then dislodge from its pan. Dust with confectioners' sugar before serving.

BAKED APPLES
WITH BREAD CRUMBS

Baked apples are the kind of out-of-fashion dessert
that upsets children and disappoints those who prefer
something more indulgent at the end of a meal. Cooked
fruits can be great, though. And stuffing them with bread
crumbs and nuts and raisins adds texture and complexity
so it isn't just mushy apples.

    Start with great apples, grown near the place you live,
in season. Firm-fleshed. Crisp. Tart, or at least with some
acidity; I like Gold Rush. Remove the stems, and use a
sharp paring knife or an apple corer to remove the core
of as many apples as you are planning on serving, leaving
the bottoms unpunctured and the apples intact. Shave off
any edible parts of the cores and mix them with Basic or
Toasted Bread Crumbs, a little sugar or honey, chopped
walnuts, raisins (rehydrated in some white wine is nice),
some orange zest and a squeeze of the orange juice, a little
cinnamon or some ground cloves, and maybe a small pinch
of salt. Work in some butter, or olive oil if you want them
to be vegan, until you have a nice wet consistency. Splash
in a little of the wine you used to rehydrate the raisins
if it is too dry. Stuff the apples with the bread crumb
mixture and place in a buttered or oiled baking dish. Add
a very light splash of white wine and bake at 360°F until
the apples are soft and cooked through and any stuffing
sticking out of the top has toasted. Serve as is—or if you
need something even more indulgent, try them with ice
cream, whipped cream, or crème Anglaise.

IRIS

The Iris is a pastry most closely associated with the pastry shops of Palermo, Sicily. Named for the opera, not the flower, it reportedly dates to 1901. Generally speaking, it is a brioche stuffed with a ricotta cream and fried. Some bakers make a fresh Sicilian-style brioche dough for their version of the pastry, but others make use of leftover rolls, which is what I have chosen to do here. Maybe you like to buy brioche rolls or milk buns at your local bakery for your hamburgers or sandwiches at home and sometimes you have too many. Usually, these aren't bread products that have a lot of life the second day. This recipe can help, and you might start buying extra rolls just to have some for this purpose. Even if you were to make this with regular leftover dinner rolls, though not ideal, it probably wouldn't be the worst thing you've put in your mouth.

Instructions

Take the rolls you didn't eat and put them in a closed bag on your counter to prevent them from drying out too much. You could even wrap them in plastic. When you want to make the Iris, take some well-drained ricotta and pass it through a fine sieve with the help of a plastic scraper, or whip it in a food processor or mixer. Mix in sugar to taste, and some small cut-up pieces of dark chocolate. Add the grated zest of an orange and a small pinch of salt. Some diced candied orange peel is nice, but not strictly necessary. Mix well and load it into a pastry bag with a wide tip and set aside.

Using a small sharp knife, carefully cut circles out of the bottom of your rolls and reserve the circles you cut out to plug the holes after it is stuffed. Using a finger, reach into the holes you made and pull out some of the crumb while leaving the roll intact. If the rolls have begun to go stale, you can moisten the insides with a little milk—but not too much. (At the shop when we make these, we use a light citrus syrup for this purpose, but most people don't have things like that around the house.) Pipe the ricotta filling into the hollowed-out rolls. You want to use a good amount; make it almost a little grotesque. Plug the holes with the reserved circles removed from the bottoms. Roll the rolls through beaten egg and then fine bread crumbs. Deep-fry around 340°–350°F somewhat slowly to give the heat enough time to penetrate to the middle and revive the roll some before the bread crumbs get too dark—a few minutes per side. This makes for a nice breakfast with your morning coffee or a snack or dessert.

Resources

This is by no means an exhaustive list, but it is a collection of places that I know, have used, and recommend. By all means, seek out and support good-quality ingredients near where you live, especially when it comes to produce.

Ingredient bundles

Bread and Salt
435 Palisade Avenue
Jersey City, NJ 07307
breadandsaltshipping.square.site

Flours

Anson Mills
1922 Gervais Street
Columbia, SC 29201
ansonmills.com

Bob's Red Mill
Available at most good grocery stores
bobsredmill.com

Carolina Ground
128 Bingham Road
Asheville, NC 28806
carolinaground.com

Castle Valley Mill
1730 Lower State Road
Doylestown, PA 18901
castlevalleymill.com

Central Milling
122 E. Center Street
Logan, UT 84321
centralmilling.com

Community Grains
5625 College Avenue
Oakland, CA 94618
communitygrains.com

Farmer Ground
240 Aiken Road
Trumansburg, NY 14886
farmergroundflour.com

Farm and Sparrow
110 Morgan Cove Road
Candler, NC 28715
farmandsparrow.com

King Arthur
135 U.S. 5 South
Norwich, VT 05055
Available at most grocery stores

Maine Grains
42 Court Street
Skowhegan, ME 04976
mainegrains.com

Wild Hive Farm
2645 Salt Point Turnpike
Clinton Corners, NY 12514
wildhivefarm.com

Cheese

Caputo Brothers Creamery
245 North Main Street #1
Spring Grove, PA 17362
caputobrotherscreamery.com

Beans

Rancho Gordo
1924 Yajome Street
Napa, CA 94559
ranchogordo.com

Italian products

Gustiamo
1715 West Farms Road
Bronx, NY 10460
www.gustiamo.com

Buon'Italia
75 9th Avenue
New York, NY 10011
buonitalia.com

Specialty produce

Melissa's Produce
melissas.com

Spices

Burlap and Barrel
burlapandbarrel.com

Acknowledgments

Rick would like to thank Melissa for writing this book. He thanks his dedicated staff and his family for their support. He'd like to thank Wild Hive Farm, Beatrice Ughi of Gustiamo, Campo Rosso Farm, and Caputo Brothers Creamery. He appreciates Drew Buzzio of Salumeria Bielese. He'd like to thank his business partners, Johnny DiPasquale and Marc Magliozzi. And thanks, as well, to Brooks Headley.

Melissa would like to thank her late father, who was alive when we started this thing. She'd like to thank her loving mother. She'd also like to thank Kate Bittman and Kerri Conan for their patience, advice, and support through this process. She is grateful for Maddy Beckwith and the Hive Mind. Thanks to Robert Sietsema and Gary He for fun restaurant adventures and lots of laughs. And she'd like to thank Rick, who says he did this for her. And thanks as well for recipe readers and testers like Annie Saunders, Joshua Siebert, Stefanie Gans, Scott Bricker, and Lena Andrews.

We'd both like to thank Mark Bittman for his years of support (and, in Melissa's case, employment); Bonnie Benwick, our marvelous recipe tester and editor; our supportive and enthusiastic editor, Tom Pold; our thoughtful and tenacious agent, Danielle Sevtcov; and our photographer, Johnny Fogg—for his incredible work and patience.

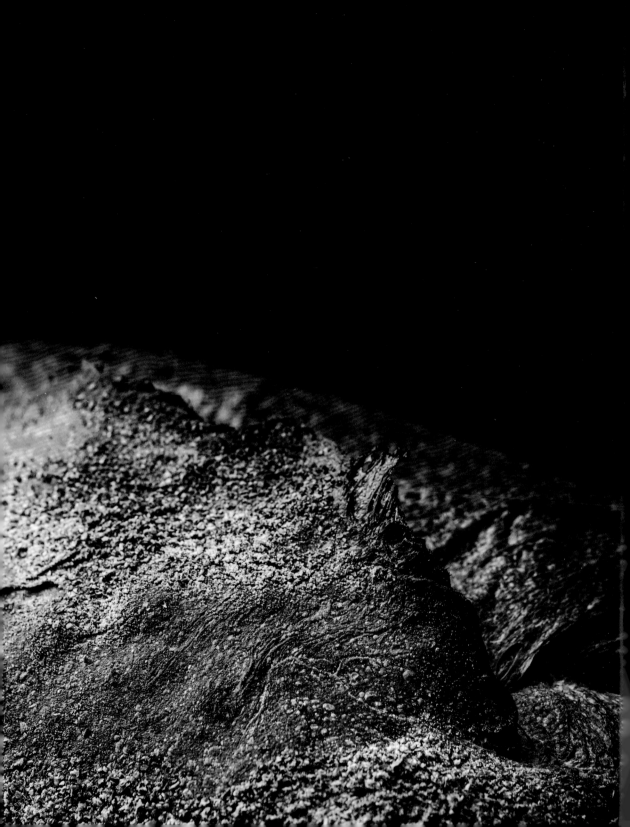

Index

Page numbers in *italics* refer to illustrations.

233

235

A NOTE ON THE TYPE

This book was set in Janson, a typeface long thought to have
been made by the Dutchman Anton Janson, who was a practicing
typefounder in Leipzig during the years 1668–1687. However, it
has been conclusively demonstrated that these types are actually
the work of Nicholas Kis (1650–1702), a Hungarian, who most
probably learned his trade from the master Dutch typefounder
Dirk Voskens. The type is an excellent example of the influential
and sturdy Dutch types that prevailed in England up to the time
William Caslon (1692–1766) developed his own incomparable
designs from them.

Composed by North Market Street Graphics, Lancaster, Pennsylvania
Printed and bound by C&C Offset, China
Designed by Anna B. Knighton

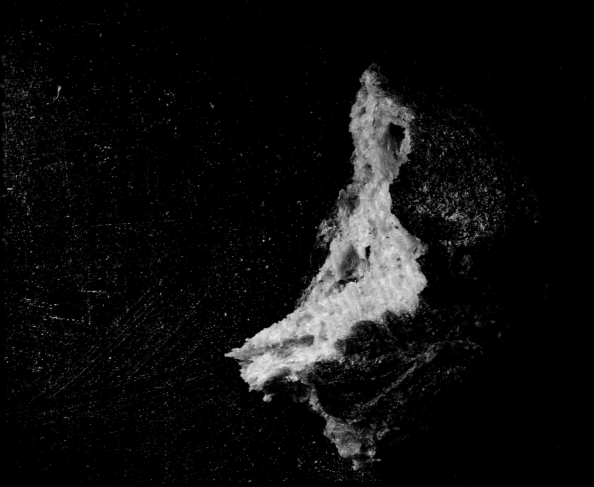